Making & Decorating
STYLISH SCREENS

Making & Decorating
STYLISH SCREENS

Katherine Duncan Aimone

LARK BOOKS

A Division of Sterling Publishing Co., Inc.
New York

DEDICATION

This book is dedicated to Ken and Ruth Aimone,
my father- and mother-in-law.

Art Director: DANA IRWIN

Photographer: SANDRA STAMBAUGH

Cover Designer: BARBARA ZARETSKY

Illustrator: OLIVIER ROLLIN

Editorial Assitance: HEATHER SMITH, VERONIKA
ALICE GUNTER, AND DELORES GOSNELL

Production Assistance: SHANNON YOKELEY,
HANNES CHAREN

Special Photography (SANOMA SYNDICATION):
OTTO POLMAN, FONS KLAPPE, PETER KOOIJMAN

ACKNOWLEDGEMENTS

Thanks to all of the wonderful designers and artists whose
works make this book a visual feast!
Kudos to Sandra Stambaugh for lending her
always-elegant eye to the photography. Thanks whole-
heartedly to Dana Irwin for her vision in finding locations,
photostyling, and designing the book. Blessings upon
Hannes Caren for being an invaluable member of the photography and production team. And, thanks as well to
Rickie Wesbrooks and Jeff Makey who demonstrated the
techniques in the front of the book. Thanks also to Andy
Rae and Mike Callahan for their patience in explaining
woodworking techniques.

And, last, but certainly not least, thanks to Rod Hubbard
who owns the Kress Condominiums in Asheville, North
Carolina, and Diane and Jim Stickney of Asheville, for
allowing us to use the beautiful locations in the book.

COVER: LISA HOUCK, *MOOD INDIGO*.1993. 66 x 90 IN.
(1.6 x 2 M). OIL ENAMEL ON WOOD.

Library of Congress Cataloging-in-Publication Data

Duncan-Aimone, Katherine.
    Making and decorating stylish screens : 30 beautiful projects / Katherine
Duncan Aimone.— 1st ed.
        p. cm.
Includes index.
ISBN 1-57990-361-4 (hard)
        1. Screens. I. Title.

TT899.45 .D85 2002
684.1—dc21   2002075227

10 9 8 7 6 5 4 3 2 1

First Edition

Published by Lark Books, a division of
Sterling Publishing Co., Inc.
387 Park Avenue South, New York, N.Y. 10016

© 2003, Lark Books

Distributed in Canada by Sterling Publishing,
c/o Canadian Manda Group, One Atlantic Ave., Suite 105
Toronto, Ontario, Canada M6K 3E7

Distributed in the U.K. by Guild of Master Craftsman Publications Ltd., Castle
Place, 166 High Street, Lewes, East Sussex, England
BN7 1XU
Tel: (+ 44) 1273 477374, Fax: (+ 44) 1273 478606, Email:
pubs@thegmcgroup.com, Web: www.gmcpublications.com

Distributed in Australia by Capricorn Link (Australia) Pty Ltd.,
P.O. Box 704, Windsor, NSW 2756 Australia

If you have questions or comments about this book, please contact:
Lark Books
67 Broadway
Asheville, NC 28801
(828) 253-0467
Manufactured In China

ISBN 1-57990-361-4

Table of Contents

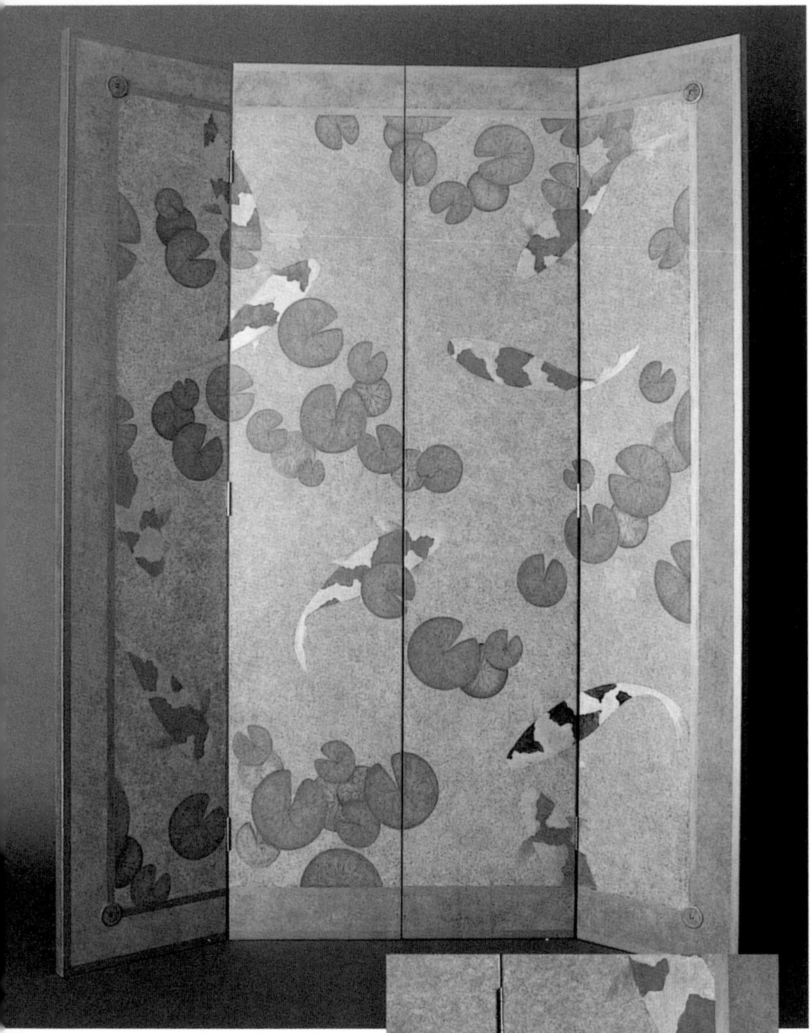

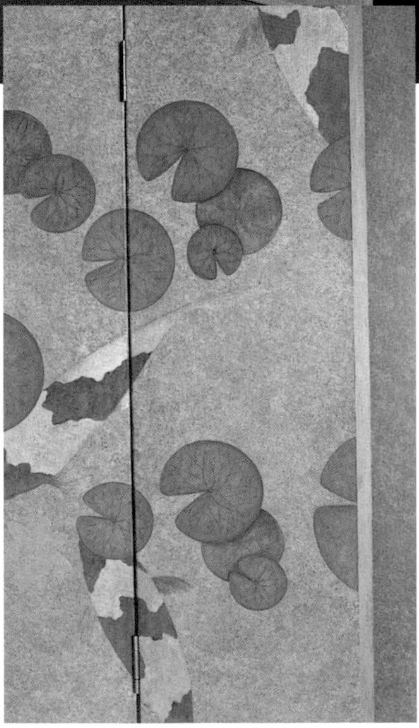

A SCREEN THAT COMBINES
THE INFLUENCE OF BOTH
CHINESE AND JAPANESE
SCREENS. CREATED BY:
WHITNEY KRUEGER,
ENCHANTED KOI. 2001.
6 X 7 FT. X 1½ IN.
(1.8 X 2.1 M X 3.8 CM).
WOOD PANELS; ACRYLIC,
GOLD LEAF, GOLD WAX,
ANTIQUE CHINESE COINS.
PHOTO BY KIM KURIAN.

INTRODUCTION

The idea of screening off an area of a home or other space is thousands of years old. The Chinese used heavy, ornate lacquered screens to divide large spaces. These tall pieces of furniture were designed for the space and were seldom moved, serving as lavish showpieces that symbolized opulence and grandeur.

The Japanese adapted the idea of decorated screens but made them lighter, crafting them from wooden lattice frames backed with paper. These screens took many forms: from starkly minimal to highly decorative. The two approaches to screens—as semi-permanent pieces of furniture versus portable pieces—remain popular today.

This book was conceived to introduce you an extremely diverse group of screen ideas: from simple fabric panels strung across an opening to ornate wallpaper and faux finish works to lightweight and revealing woven wire pieces. You'll also discover a number of ways to use all sorts of found materials—from rustic twigs and branches to corrugated metal and salvaged doors—to create screens with character and originality.

Today's definition of screens has been loosened to include banners and lightweight framed pieces that are hung at strategic points in a room to create a visual break while serving as engaging works of art. Small tabletop artworks referencing the accordion-like shape of traditional screens are also included.

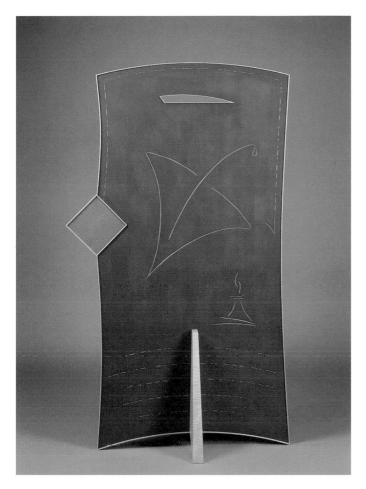 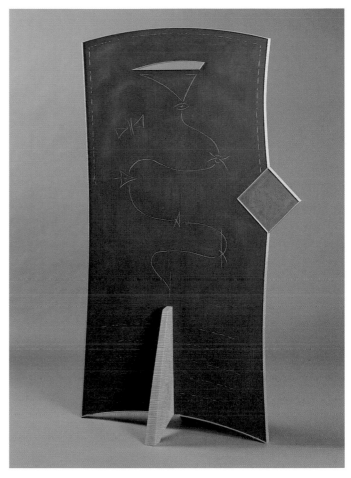

A FREESTANDING SCREEN SERVES AS BOTH A TWO-DIMENSIONAL AND THREE-DIMENSIONAL WORK OF ART. CREATED BY: MARK DEL GUIDICE, *...SWEET SORROW*. 2002. 73 x 41 x 18 IN. (183 x 103 x 45 CM). SCREEN CONSTRUCTED FROM CURLY MAPLE, FIBERBOARD; SURFACE: MILK PAINT, VARNISH; INCISED AND CARVED WITH MORSE CODE AND PERSONAL INTUITIVE HIEROGLYPHS. PHOTO BY CLEMENTS/HOWCROFT.

A TABLETOP SCREEN DOUBLES AS AN INTRIGUING WORK OF ART. CREATED BY: LISA WILLIAMSON, *HOT SWING SONG*. 2000. 21 x 49 IN. (52.5 x 122.5 CM). ACRYLIC ON WOOD. PHOTO BY ARTIST.

WALLPAPERED SCREEN (SEE PROJECT ON PAGE **24**).

A COLORFUL HANGING PANEL SERVES AS A VISUAL BREAK IN A ROOM (SEE PROJECT ON PAGE **120**).

The front section of this book introduces you to a couple of key ways to make screen substrates from wooden panels and open frames. The panels are a lot like blank canvases waiting to be filled with paint, stamping, wallpaper, collage, or any medium of your choice. The frames can be upholstered, woven with various materials, or stretched with sheer fabric to create enchanting pieces that reveal as much as they conceal. You can make and decorate as many panels and frames as you need to make a hinged screen that fits your purposes.

You can also purchase readymade screens that allow you to add your own fabric or paper panels that can be changed out. With this simple approach, you can create a screen without having to deal with building a frame. This book also shows you ways to alter a simple paper-backed screen, giving you more choices for decorating screens with minimal fuss.

Each project in the book gives you complete instructions on how to make it from start to finish. You won't

OLD CORRUGATED TIN IS MADE INTO A STYLISH SCREEN
(SEE PROJECT PAGE **64**).

PAINTED SILK PANELS HUNG ON A READY-MADE METAL FRAME
(SEE PROJECT ON PAGE **108**).

have to guess. The materials and tools are listed in the order that you'll use them as you make the screen and are readily available at a nominal cost through home supply, craft, or art stores.

Keep in mind that you can alter any of the project ideas to suit your purposes by making them wider or taller or changing the design and color. If you don't like the shape of the panel suggested in the project, simply make up your own. There are as many shapes for wooden panels as you can dream up, and this part of the

design is as important as the surface decoration that you choose.

At the end of the book, you'll find an enticing gallery section filled with work created by furniture designers, craftspeople, artists, and sculptors. This section will show you the great variety of screens that are being made today for homes, galleries, offices, and public places.

Making screens can require as little as a small table in a room or as much as a garage or shop with woodworking tools. Where you work and how is really a matter of common sense and preference. The variety of projects in this book gives you many choices.

Whether you're cutting wood or not, you'll need a well-ventilated area with open floor space for working on a larger screen. A large work surface (such as a workbench) is ideal, although you can use the floor for decorating screens if you don't have one. If you're painting or stamping several panels that relate to one another, you might find that you prefer working on the floor where you can get a bigger picture of what you're doing. You can also lean panels against a wall that you've protected with paper or a suspended drop cloth.

But if you're doing basic carpentry or working in detail, it will probably be necessary to place the panels on a workbench. Sawhorses and plywood, or a couple of large tables butted together, can be used for basic carpentry and for decorating the panels of your screen.

You can set up a basic woodworking shop in your garage or basement without a lot of fuss. (If you don't have an appropriate space for

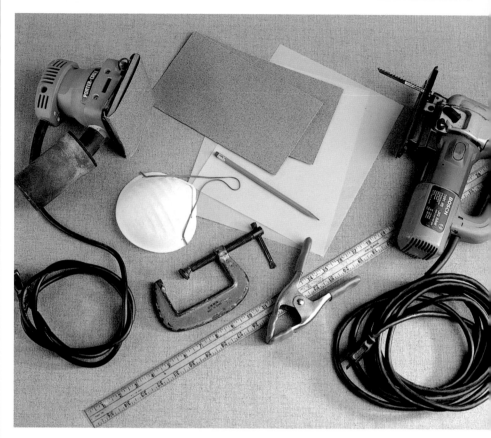

BASIC WOODWORKING TOOLS CAN BE USED TO MAKE SIMPLE SCREENS. *LEFT TO RIGHT:* SANDER AND SANDPAPER, PAPER FOR CREATING TEMPLATES, JIGSAW, CLAMPS, STRAIGHTEDGE, DUST MASK

this, you can always cut and assemble wood outside when the weather is good, then store your equipment inside.) With some basic tools such as clamps, a simple handsaw and miter box (for cutting straight edges), a jigsaw (for cutting curves), sandpaper (for smoothing curves), and an electric drill/screwdriver (for hinging), you can create most of the wooden screens in this book.

Make sure to wear protective gear such as glasses and a mask when you're cutting and sanding, particu-

larly if you're working with fiberboard. If you're doing a lot of sawing, it is helpful to have a power vacuum cleaner to clean up the sawdust after you've finished.

In most cases, it makes sense to leave the panels or frames of your screen unhinged until you've embellished them. All of the projects in this book were created in that way. Keep the overall design of the screen and how the panels will ultimately relate to one another in mind as you work.

MAKING SCREENS: WOODEN PANELS AND FRAMES

The following section will guide you through the rudimentary steps of making solid-panel screens in any shape of your choice that can then be decorated. You'll also learn how to make basic frames that can be filled with paper, fabric, ribbon, or other materials. Many of the projects in this book utilize one of these options.

MAKING A SOLID-PANEL SCREEN

Plywood can be cut to any size and shape to make solid-panel screens. To make screen panels, we suggest that you use a high-grade, hardwood plywood. Plywoods come in standard 4 x 8-foot (1.2 x 2.4 m) sheets that can be cut to the sizes you need. The tops of these panels can be cut into shapes that are as basic or ornamental as you like. If you plan to decorate the back as well, you'll need to buy plywood with two smooth sides.

Keep in mind that the thicker the plywood is, the heavier it's going to be to move around. The projects in this book use ¾-inch (1.9 cm) plywood which is a heavy plywood that is thick enough to be stable and not warp easily when cut into large pieces. You can also use medium-density fiberboard (MDF), which is a composite board. It maintains its shape well but is

incredibly heavy. If you use it, consider making smaller screens or screens that you don't plan to move around very often.

If your screen idea calls for large surfaces, solid panels are the way to go. The possibilities for decoration are endless—painting, stamping, stenciling, wallpapering, collage, and decoupage are among the many options.

CUTTING THE PANELS

You'll need some basic woodworking tools, and you may need some help with lifting to cut these panels that involve no joinery—simply cutting, sanding, priming, and hinging. Below are the tools you'll need and steps to follow.

MATERIALS AND TOOLS

Sheets of high-grade plywood or medium-density fiberboard (MDF)

Workbench (a couple of sawhorses with a large piece of plywood on top) or flat surface suitable for clamping wood

C-clamps

Template for decorative top (optional)

Long metal straightedge

Measuring tape

Dust mask

Jigsaw

Medium and fine-grit sandpaper

Small electric sander (optional)

Wood primer

Paintbrush

INSTRUCTIONS

• To cut each panel, place the plywood or fiberboard on your work surface and clamp it into place (photo 1).

1

• Position the template at the top of the panel, and trace around it (photo 2). Use the metal straightedge to extend the lines of the template to create the length of your panel. (You can adjust this length as you wish).

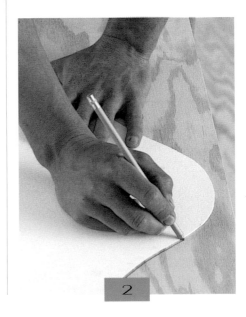

2

• Slide the panel out so that the top hangs over the edge of your work surface. Put on the dust mask. Place the jigsaw blade along the top line, beginning at a corner. Hold it firmly with the blade perpendicular to the surface, and gently begin to cut (photo 3). Hold it as steady as possible, and move slowly. (Small imperfections in the cutting can be sanded away later.) As needed, cut

outward and away from the line to remove pieces of wood. Or, if you get stuck at some point, approach the line from another direction.

• After you've cut around the top, cut down the straight side. Repeat this on the other side, and cut off the bottom straight edge of the panel, adjusting the wood on the table and reclamping it as needed.

• Use medium-grit sandpaper to sand away the rough edges until fairly

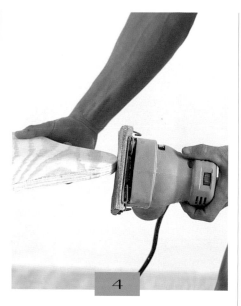

smooth (photo 4). (You can do this without a sander, but it makes it easier if you use one.) Then follow up with the fine-grit sandpaper to round the edges

by hand until you are satisfied with their consistency and smoothness.

• Apply a coat of wood primer to the surface before decorating it (photo 5).

WOODEN PANELS CAN BE CUT TO ANY SHAPE OF YOUR CHOICE AND DECORATED WITH VARIOUS FINISHES (TO MAKE THIS FAUX FINISH SCREEN, SEE PROJECT ON PAGE 30).

MAKING FRAME SCREENS

Simple open frames can be filled with materials to make visually inspiring screens. From a single frame suspended from the ceiling, to several ones hinged together, frames are a natural choice for creating screens that add an aesthetic touch and a visual "break" to a room without completely concealing the objects behind them.

You may choose to make an artistic interpretation such as the screen project on page 94, which allows the areas behind it to be almost totally visible through a web of wire, or the project on page 112 that capitalizes on the seductive beauty of sheer fabric.

Unlike heavy panel screens that provide a wonderful flat surface for painting or applying other surface decoration, open frames allow light to enhance the texture and color of paper, the shiny properties of beads, or the beauty of woven fabric.

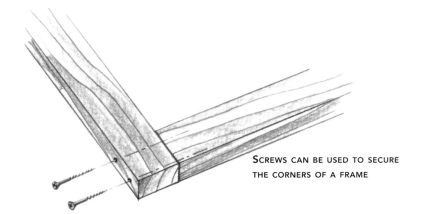

SCREWS CAN BE USED TO SECURE THE CORNERS OF A FRAME

You can make your own frame screens with a variety of joinery techniques that range from simple to complex (see photo below). The simplest joinery technique is accomplished with wood screws, which are adequate for most purposes. Several other joinery techniques are pictured and briefly described as well, although detailed instructions are not given. If you want to use one of the more complicated joinery options, they are standard to woodworking books.

The frames can be made in any height and width of your choice.

Hinging as few as two frames together will allow your screen to stand, as long as it is wide enough in proportion to its height that it doesn't topple over. To finish the screen before adding the materials inside it, you can paint it, stain it, wax it, or simply apply a couple of coats of acrylic varnish.

USING SCREWS TO SECURE A FRAME

The simplest frame can be made with wood screws and readily available hand tools that are listed below. Even if you've never worked with wood before, you can make this frame without a lot of fuss. You can adjust the width of the wood pieces to fit your preferences. The frame that we made below is simply an example.

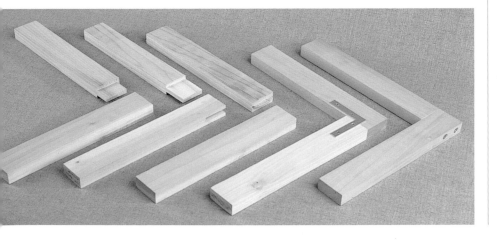

CORNERS FOR FRAMES CAN BE ASSEMBLED WITH A VARIETY OF JOINERY THAT RANGES FROM SIMPLE WOOD SCREWS TO MORTISE-AND-TENON JOINERY.
RIGHT TO LEFT:
CONVENTIONAL WOOD SCREW JOINERY, CORNER BRACKET JOINERY, BISCUIT JOINERY, SLIP JOINT/OPEN MORTISE-AND-TENON JOINERY, BASIC MORTISE-AND-TENON WITH SHOULDER ON THREE SIDES

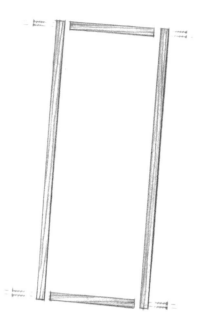

MATERIALS AND TOOLS FOR FRAME SCREENS

Lengths of untreated soft wood (for most of the frames in this book, we used ¾ x 1¼-inch [1.9 x 3.2 cm] pieces to make a 20½ x 64-inch [52.1 cm x 1.6 m] frame [outside dimensions] out of two 18-inch [45.7 cm] crosspieces and two 64-inch [1.6 m] side pieces)

Metal ruler or measuring tape

Small carpenter's square

C-clamps

Handheld saw

Miter box (optional)

Medium-grit sandpaper

Electric drill/screwdriver with bits, including countersink drill bit to fit your screws

4 brass wood screws (we used #10 x 2½ inches [6.4 cm])

INSTRUCTIONS

• To make a rectangular frame, measure and mark off two identical wood pieces that equal the height of the panel you wish to make (these will be the sides of the frame). To determine the width of the frame's two crosspieces, subtract twice the width of the wooden lengths from the width that you want for your frame. Use the carpenter's square to guide you in marking sawing lines on the crosspieces that are exactly perpendicular to the length of the wood pieces.

• Clamp each piece of wood along the long edge of your workbench, adjusting it so that each sawing line protrudes slightly beyond the end, allowing you to saw off the excess length. Or, if you're using a miter box, set it to 90°, and saw the pieces.

• Sand the ends of the pieces as needed.

• To mark the positions for the screws, place one of the crosspieces at a right angle to one of the long pieces, making sure that the edges are aligned at the top. Extend the inside line of the crosspiece across the width of the longer piece, and down the narrow edge. Within this area, mark two Xs indicating where you'll place the screws. Use this process to mark off the remaining three connecting corners.

• Align a crosspiece and a side of the frame on the corner of your work surface, and clamp them into place.

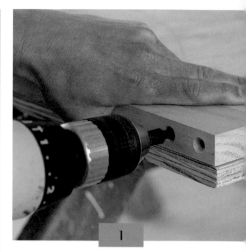

Attach a countersink drill bit to your drill that fits your screws. Drill carefully until you have two indentations into which the heads of your screws will sit neatly (photo 1).

• Use a drill bit that is slightly larger than your screw to drill clearance holes through the indentations you've already drilled. (DO NOT drill into the crosspiece at this point.)

• Next you'll drill corresponding pilot holes in the end of the crosspiece. Attach a drill bit to the drill that is slightly smaller than the screw, and drill through the two countersink holes into the crosspiece (photo 2).

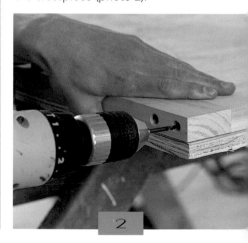

- Attach a screwdriver bit that fits your screws, and use it to attach the two pieces with the wood screws (photo 3).

- Repeat these steps to secure the remaining other three corners of your frame.

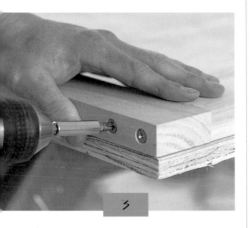

HINGING THE PANELS

Whether you're hinging together heavy panels or lightweight frames, double-acting/butterfly hinges are ideal for screens because they allow the panels to move easily in both directions and fold together accordion-style. In other words, you'll have the freedom to vary the position of the panels to fit the needs of your space. These hinges come in different sizes, so choose those that fit the narrow edges of your screen panels. (Since we consistently used ¾-inch [1.9 cm] plywood or fiberboard and frames with a ¾-inch [1.9 cm] narrow edge, we used hinges measuring ¾ x 1¾ inches [1.9 x 4.4 cm]).

If you're using old hinges or decorative hinges because you like the way they look, you'll need to be conscious of the direction that the panels will fold after the hinges are in place. If you want to be able to fold up the screen accordion-style, you'll need to alternate the position of the hinges between panels.

How many hinges you use between panels depends on the strength of the hinges, the height and weight of your panels, and your aesthetic preferences. In general, you'll probably only need two hinges between panels for an average-sized screen that measures 4 to 6 feet (1.2 to 1.8 m) in height. If you're using only two hinges, space the hinges a practical and attractive distance from the top and the bottom of the panels that they're joining. If you're using three hinges, center the third hinge between the two hinges. If the panels are tall and heavy, they may demand more hinges. (For instance, the tall upholstered screen on page 44 is hinged with four hinges between each.)

To hinge together two panels with double-acting/butterfly hinges, you'll need a drill fitted with a bit to make pilot holes (a bit that is slightly smaller than your screws) and a bit driver that matches the head of your screws. To begin, place two of the panels of your screens together

HINGING TOOLS: AN ELECTRIC DRILL/SCREWDRIVER, A REGULAR SCREWDRIVER, STRAIGHTEDGE, AND HINGES

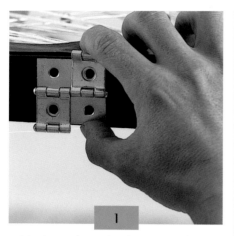

1

with the right sides facing each other.

Make certain the bottoms and sides of the panels are perfectly aligned. Slide a thin piece of cardboard (about ⅛ inch [3 mm]) between the panels to create space for the center part of the hinge when you mark the drill holes. Position the hinge, and mark the holes (photo 1).

Use the drill fitted with the smaller bit to make pilot holes in the frame or panel (photo 2). Reposition the

2

hinge on top of the pilot holes, and use the screwdriver to attach the screws, making sure that they go in straight (photo 3). When you are finished, the hinge should be perfectly aligned with the edges of the frame, with the outer hinges overlapping slightly, as shown (photo 4). Continue this process to add other hinges to your panels as needed.

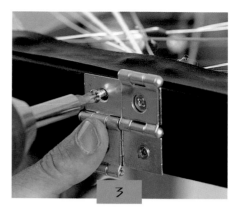

3

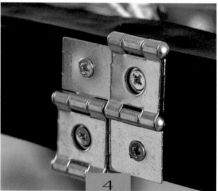

4

A MEDUIM-SIZED SCREEN CAN BE HINGED WITH TWO HINGES BETWEEN EACH PANEL (SEE PROJECT ON PAGE **152**).

FABRIC AND UPHOLSTERY SCREENS

Whether you're using a ready-made screen with open sections made for adding fabric panels, or you're covering frames that you've made yourself, there are many ways to use fabric to decorate screens.

The most obvious way is upholstery, but you can also emboss or paint fabric and sew it into panels that fit a screen (see the projects on pages

most complex technique in this book that utilizes fabric is upholstery, which is described in easy-to-follow steps below.

UPHOLSTERING FRAMES

Open wooden frames can be transferred into panels that conceal. They provide a sturdy and relatively lightweight armature that looks solid once it is covered in fabric. Needless to say, your choices for screen design are unlimited when

The following example of upholstering a single frame tells you what you'll need and illustrates the basics. For this sample, we used a smaller frame that didn't need reinforcing crosspieces.

MATERIALS AND TOOLS

Open frame

Polyester batting (low loft), enough to amply cover both sides of the frame

Staple gun

¼-inch (6 mm) staples

Tack hammer

Fabric scissors

1 x 32-inch (2.5 x 81.2 cm) polyester batting, enough to fill the inside dimensions of the frame

Sewing needle with hole large enough to accommodate thread

Spool of black heavy-duty thread

Upholstery fabric that measures at least the length and width of the frame plus 4 inches (10.2 cm) in both directions

Pushpins

PVA acid-free glue made for paper or fabric

⅝-inch (1.6 cm) flat artist's paintbrush

Trim in color that matches your fabric, long enough to go around the edge of the frame with a width that is within ⅛ inch (3 mm) of the width of the frame's narrow edge

FABRIC, BATTING, STAPLE GUN, AND FINISHING RIBBON FOR UPHOLSTERY

40 and 108), weave ribbons on a frame that you've made (see the project on page 100), or sew colorful banners that can be suspended to divide a room (see the project on page 120). One of our designers found a unique way to use several woven textiles that she bought on a vacation by designing a screen that she had fabricated from steel (see page 76).

In essence, the screen provides a vehicle for displaying the fabric while serving the dual purpose of blocking off an area of a room. The

you look at the many choices of fabrics.

If you're making a larger frame that will eventually be upholstered or covered, you may want to add reinforcing crosspieces (braces) inside the width of the frame, as we did for the project on page 44. To do this, simply cut more wood pieces of the same length, and screw them into place with the same system that you would use to attach crosspieces at the top and bottom. (As described in making frame screens).

• Place the frame on your work surface, and drape the low-loft polyester batting over the frame and center it.

• Place the staple gun in the center of one of the long sides. Attach the batting with a few staples in the center that are spaced at least 2 inches (5 cm) apart (photo 1). Use the tack hammer as needed to reinforce the staples.

• Move to the center of the top of the frame, and staple the center of this area, stretching it lightly. Staple the batting to the other two centers of the remaining

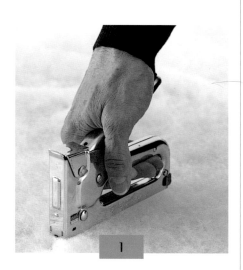

side and bottom of the frame.

• After you've stapled the batting in the center portions of each side of the frame, work your way around the frame to staple the remaining edges in place. Use scissors to trim away the excess batting (photo 2).

• Turn the frame over. From the 1-inch-

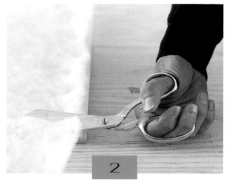

wide (2.5 cm) batting, cut two pieces that fit inside the two open spaces of the frame (photo 3). Press them into place so that they fill the frame and lie smooth and flat (photo 4).

• Staple low-loft batting to the other

side of the frame as you did in the previous steps.

• Stand one of the frames in an open doorway or upright on its side on your worktable. Thread the sewing needle with a 3-yard (2.7 m) length of the black

thread. Beginning in one of the corners of the frame, use long stitches to sew a very large "X" through the layers of batting to hold them in place (photo 5). Secure the ends of the thread with knots, and cut off the excess thread. (Remember that these threads won't show, they're only there to prevent the

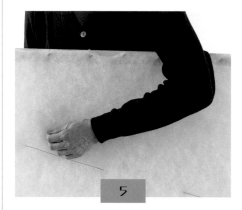

batting from sagging or shifting later on.)

• Place the fabric facedown on your work surface. Fold the fabric in half along the width, and cut it along the fold so that you have two long pieces of the same size (photo 6).

• Place one of the frames along the length of the upholstery fabric, and hold it in place temporarily with push-pins (photo 7). Flip it over, and check

7

the orientation of the fabric, particularly if you're using a pattern. Remove the pins, leaving the fabric underneath.

• Beginning at the top of your fabric, stretch it over the side of the frame. Staple it first in the CENTER on the narrow edge on a long side, placing the staple close to THE FAR EDGE (so that you'll be able to easily place the hinges in the center later without hitting staples). Place staples in the center of each side to secure the fabric, stretching it slightly as you do this.

• Lightly pull the fabric to each side of the staples you've placed, and staple the fabric into place, working from the center out. Use the tack hammer to reinforce the staples as needed (photo 8).

8

• When you reach a corner, fold the fabric under to hide it (photo 9). Repeat this process to staple the fabric to the sides, lining up your staples along the far edges of the sides of each frame so that the center is free for placing hinges later.

9

• Flip the frame over, and attach another piece of fabric to the other side in exactly the same way, keeping the orientation of the fabric in mind so that it works with the front.

10

• Upholster as many frames as you wish to use for your screen, following the procedure outlined above. After you've finished, hinge the panels together as described in the previous section.

• After the panels are hinged, use the glue to apply pieces of ribbon around the edges (photo 10), working around the hinges (see the project on page 44 for more detail about this process).

A LARGE UPHOLSTERED SCREEN PROVIDES AN EFFECTIVE VISUAL BARRIER (SEE PROJECT ON PAGE **44**).

DECORATING SCREENS

Decorating the surfaces of blank panels to create an original screen is like making a work of art. Whether you like to paint, draw, stamp, stencil, decoupage, collage, wallpaper, or combine different media, you can enhance screens with almost anything that will stick to the surface! This book presents you with lots of projects that will give you inspiration in this area (for examples, see the projects on pages 36, 50, and 124).

When you're working with wooden panels as your substrate, always prepare the surface with wood primer or another type of sealer before you begin (if you want the wood to show through, you can use a clear acrylic wood sealer). Then you're free to work on the surface with a variety of media.

OTHER SCREEN OPTIONS

There are many other choices for creating screens that don't use wooden panels or frames. For instance, you'll find lots of screens on the market that can be altered or filled with panels made from materials of your choice.

You can also take advantage of salvage materials such as old doors and windows to make interesting screens, or lash together twigs or other natural materials to make both outdoor and indoor screens.

Use your imagination while scouting for unusual materials that can be adapted to make screens. This book is only the beginning—when you start looking for them, you'll see more and more possibilities.

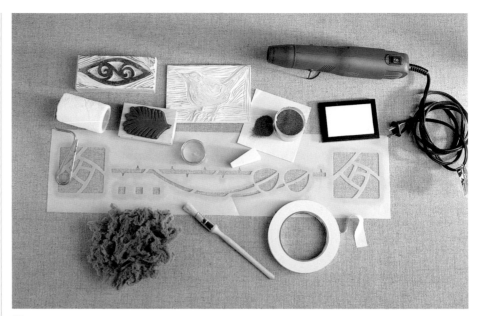

MATERIALS AND TOOLS FOR SURFACE DECORATION. *LEFT TO RIGHT*: STAMPS AND ROLLER, EMBOSSING INK AND POWDERS, EMBOSSING HEAT TOOL, STENCIL AND STENCIL BRUSH, COSMETIC SPONGE, MASKING TAPE, SEA SPONGE

TRANSFORMING READY-MADE SCREENS

There are many possibilities for creating unique screens that don't involve making the screen first. For example, you can alter a Japanese-style paper screen by cutting out sections and replacing them with handmade papers that have been decorated with stamping or other media (see the projects on pages 50 and 53).

You can also purchase both wooden and metal screens with empty spaces that are made to be filled with paper or fabric panels. Several projects in this book explore the possibilities for this idea. Then you can concentrate on designing and preparing the panels with painting, stamping, embossing, or other surface decoration techniques.

WALLPAPER IS IDEAL FOR DECORATING SCREENS

ALTER A PAPER SCREEN WITH STAMPED AND EMBOSSED PAPERS

Another idea along these lines is using lightweight hollow-core doors from a home supply store. They're relatively inexpensive and can be painted or embellished with anything you choose. Then, all you'll have to deal with is hinging them. (Apply a coat of primer to them before painting, stamping, or collaging them.)

USING NATURAL AND RECYCLED MATERIALS

Outdoor as well as indoor screens can be assembled from natural materials such as twigs, sticks, and bamboo (see the section called Naturally Influenced that begins on page 134). The inherent flaws and inconsistencies of the materials are a large part of the charm of using them. For instance, one of our designers always finds an excuse to use

discarded sticks in her work that she searches for in the woods near her home. The distinctive and random teeth marks left by beavers become a part of the visual charm of her work.

OLD WOODEN DOORS ARE PAINTED AND DISTRESSED TO MAKE A UNIQUE DIVIDER (SEE PROJECT ON PAGE 60).

Look around the woods of your own area, and you may find that you'll come up with your own ideas for using natural materials to build or enhance screens.

Scavenging for man-made materials can also lend you lots of ideas. Old doors, windows, roof tin, ceiling tiles, and other building materials can be recycled into artful screens that are inherently interesting because of their worn properties. (See the section called Recycled and Altered that begins on page 58.)

Visit old lumber and metal yards to find the great stuff that's been left out in the weather. You may save it from going to the dump and find a treasure that no

one else has recognized. Thrift stores are also great places to find those borderline things that don't fit into an immediately usable or salable category, such as piles of old doors or broken windows. Trendy salvage stores will charge you a lot more money, since you're paying someone else to scavenge for you, but you can also find great bargains there too. Large antique stores or warehouses are also a source for such items.

Once you've found your materials, you can leave them as they are, or paint and distress them to look a certain way. Both of these ideas are covered in this book.

THE PROJECTS

ESSENTIALLY, A SCREEN CAN BE AS SIMPLE AS A DECORATIVE PIECE OF FABRIC STRUNG ON A CORD THAT DIVIDES A ROOM OR AS COMPLEX AS A MOVEABLE WALL DIVIDER ON WHEELS. THE PROJECTS ON THE FOLLOWING PAGES PRESENT A WIDE RANGE OF CHOICES FOR MAKING SCREENS THAT RANGE FROM EASY TO COMPLEX. MANY ARE UNCONVENTIONAL AND IMAGINATIVE, WHILE OTHERS ARE ELEGANT AND TRADITIONAL.

FOLLOW OUR INSTRUCTIONS OR COME UP WITH VARIATIONS OF YOUR OWN, KEEPING IN MIND THAT YOU CAN ALWAYS ADJUST THE HEIGHT AND WIDTH OF PANELS OR FRAMES TO SUIT THE PURPOSES OF YOUR SPACE. REFER BACK TO THE FRONT SECTION OF THE BOOK WHEN YOU NEED HELP WITH MAKING PANELS, FRAMES, OR HINGING A SCREEN.

OUR SCREENS ARE LOOSELY DIVIDED INTO TRADITIONAL AND FUNCTIONAL, RECYCLED AND ALTERED, AIRY AND REVEALING, AND NATURALLY INFLUENCED. WHATEVER YOUR PURPOSE FOR A SCREEN—WHETHER IT IS TO DIVIDE A ROOM OR GARDEN, HIDE A CORNER, OR SIMPLY SHOW OFF YOUR SKILLS IN PAINTING AND DECORATING— WE HOPE THAT YOU FIND THE PROCESS OF MAKING A SCREEN AS EXCITING AND REWARDING AS WE DID.

TRADITIONAL AND FUNCTIONAL

  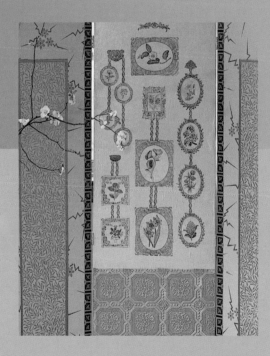

COVER A THREE-PANELED SCREEN WITH EXQUISITE WALLPAPERS OR EMBOSS VELVET WITH STAMPS TO MAKE A RICH-LOOKING FABRIC SCREEN. MAKE A TALL, SLIM UPHOLSTERED SCREEN OR A COZY FIRE SCREEN STENCILED WITH DESIGNS. THIS SECTION PRESENTS YOU WITH ELEGANT EXAMPLES OF SCREENS THAT CAN BE USED TO ENHANCE OR DIVIDE A ROOM.

DESIGNER
LYNA FARKAS

VICTORIAN-STYLE WALLPAPER SCREEN

USE VARIOUS WALLPAPERS TO CREATE A GORGEOUS, NOSTALGIC SCREEN THAT FEATURES A PRINT GALLERY ON THE CENTRAL PANEL, ACCOMPANIED BY COMPLEMENTARY FLANKING PANELS.

Materials & Tools

2 sheets of ¾-inch (1.9 cm) x 4 x 8-foot (1.2 x 2.4 m) smooth plywood

Sawhorses with large piece of plywood or other large work surface

Panel template (see fig. 1 on page 28)

Jigsaw

C-clamps

Fine- and medium-grit sandpaper

Small handheld sander (optional)

Tack cloth

Drop cloth

2 paint rollers with ¼-inch-wide (6 mm) nap

Paint trays with disposable liners

Latex primer

Gold latex paint (enough to paint the backs of the panels)

Sharp paper scissors

Long metal straightedge

Wallpaper liner (enough to cover the three panels)

4-inch-wide (10.2 cm) paintbrush to apply paste

Wallpaper paste

Wallpaper smoothing brush

Kitchen sponge

Carpenter's level

Craft knife with several sharp blades

CONTINUED ON NEXT PAGE

Instructions

1. Cut out three 18-inch-wide (45.7 cm) long panels from your plywood. On your work surface, use the jigsaw to cut out the wood panels following the panel template for the top cuts (see pages 11 and 12 for detailed instructions about cutting). Make your screen a height of your choice—ours measures 5½ feet (1.7 m) at the highest point.

2. Lightly sand the front and back of each panel. Wipe down the panels with the tack cloth to remove the dust.

3. Spread out the drop cloth on your work surface or floor.

4. Use the ¼-inch (6 mm) nap roller to apply primer to the sides and backs of the screen's panels, and allow it to dry. Apply primer to the fronts of the panels.

5. With a clean ¼-inch (6 mm) nap roller, roll two coats of gold paint on the sides and backs of the panels, allowing the paint to dry between coats. Flip the panels over after they are dry.

6. Use scissors and the straightedge to cut out three pieces of identical pieces of wallpaper liner to fit the front (unpainted side) of each panel. Set one of the pieces aside for later.

7. Use the 4-inch-wide (10.2 cm) paintbrush to brush wallpaper paste onto the back of one of the pieces of lining paper, making sure that you cover the entire back of the paper with the paste.

8. Fold over the top and bottom ends of the paper, paste-to-paste, so that they meet close to the center. Allow the paste to set for a couple of minutes. (This is known as "booking.")

9. Unfold the upper half of the paper while leaving the lower fold in place. Hold the unfolded edge between your thumb and fingers, and position it along the top of the panel. Slide the wallpaper into position.

10. Use the smoothing brush to

press the paper against the panel, brushing down the center and firmly toward the edges. Unfold the lower half of the paper, and brush it against the panel.

1 1 . Remove any air bubbles under the paper by carefully lifting the nearest corner of the paper and rebrushing it against the panel. Dampen the sponge, and use it to wipe away excess paste from around the edges of the paper.

1 2 . Repeat steps 7 through 11 to place liner paper on the front of another panel.

1 3 . Once the liner is in place, cut two identical pieces of the background wallpaper to fit the front of each flanking panel. Paste the wallpaper to the panels following the same procedure that you used for the liner.

1 4 . From another wallpaper, cut two identical rectangular pieces of wallpaper that fit down the middle of the two flanking panels. From the same wallpaper, cut out pieces that fit the triangular crest of all three panels. Set one of the triangular pieces aside for later.

1 5 . Find the center of each flanking panel, and use the level and ruler to lightly draw two hori-

zontal lines to mark the position of each of the rectangular pieces. Paste and apply the pieces to each flanking panel between the lines.

1 6 . Paste and apply the triangular pieces to the crests of the flanking panels.

1 7 . Next, you'll cut and apply a 1-inch (2.5 cm) frame-like border around each of the rectangular pieces that you applied in step 15. Cut two pieces for each vertical side and two for each horizontal side, adding 6 inches (15.2 cm) to each measurement.

1 8 . Paste the backs of the strips, leaving about 3 inches (7.6 cm) unpasted on each end. Smooth the strips into place around the rectangular panels like a frame, overlapping the ends.

1 9 . Where the strips overlap at each corner, use the straightedge to lightly draw a diagonal. Use the craft knife to carefully cut the strips along each of these lines. Butt the ends of the border strips together as you smooth them firmly into place with a damp sponge. Wipe away any excess paste.

2 0 . Measure and cut 2-inch (5.1 cm) border strips to fit around the outer edges of the two flanking

MATERIALS & TOOLS

Wallpapers of your choice: one to serve as the background for two flanking panels, another to overlay on the flanking panels as rectangular shapes so as to cover the crests of the panels, goldpaper for framing the flanking panels, paper with border to use for edging the flanking panels, patterned paper for the upper section of the central panel, embossed wallpaper for the bottom half of the central panel

Black-and-white photocopied images from copyright-free books for central panel (We used images and designs that complemented the wallpapers, photocopied prints of frames and borders, and images to use as links such as ropes and swags.)

Piece of glass or other hard surface for cutting out paper images with the craft knife

Small paper scissors

Plastic container for mixing paint

Artist's acrylic paint in raw umber

3-inch-wide (7.6 cm) paintbrush

Artist's low-tack masking tape

4 double-acting/butterfly hinges with screws, each hinge measuring ¾ x 1¾ inches (1.9 x 4.4 cm)

panels, following step 17. Repeat steps 18 and 19 to paste them and miter the edges.

2 1 . Paste the third piece of liner in place on front of the central, remaining panel.

2 2 . Cut out a piece of the patterned wallpaper to fit the upper two-thirds of the panel (not the crest). Paste the paper in place on the panel.

2 3 . Paste the triangular piece of paper that you cut out in step 14 onto the crest of the central panel, so that it butts against the patterned wallpaper.

2 4 . Cut a 1-inch (2.5 cm) strip from the gold wallpaper that fits over the seam where the top and middle papers meet. Paste it into place over the seam.

2 5 . Cut out a piece from the embossed wallpaper that fits the bottom section of the panel plus about an inch (2.5 cm). Paste the paper to the panel so the top edge overlaps the bottom edge of the middle paper.

2 6 . Apply a coat of gold latex paint with the nap roller to the embossed wallpaper. When the paint has dried, apply a second coat.

2 7 . Set the black and white prints, frames, and linking pieces on your hard cutting surface, and trim them with the craft knife or small paper scissors.

2 8 . Make a wash for the cutout pieces (to create a sepia look) by mixing two parts of acrylic raw umber paint with one part water in the plastic container. Use the 3-inch-wide (7.6 cm) paintbrush to apply the wash, and allow it to dry.

2 9 . Position the images, frames, and links as you wish on top of the central panel. Move them around until you achieve the look you want, using low-tack masking tape to hold them in place. Step back and look at the panel to make sure that the pieces are level and spaced as you wish.

3 0 . Starting with the outermost pieces, remove each one at a time, and apply a thin coat of paste to the back before repositioning them. Press the pieces around the edges with a damp sponge, removing excess paste. Apply the remaining pieces the same way.

3 1 . Hinge the screen (see pages 15 and 16 for instructions).

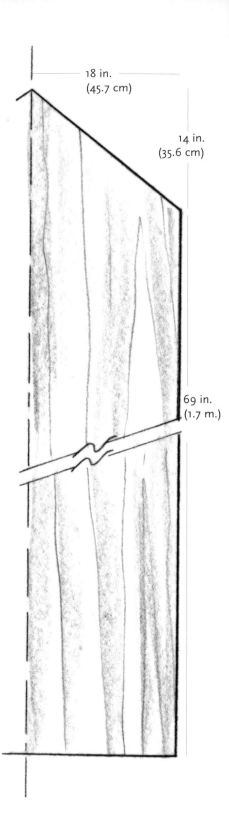

18 in.
(45.7 cm)

14 in.
(35.6 cm)

69 in.
(1.7 m.)

Figure 1

Gallery

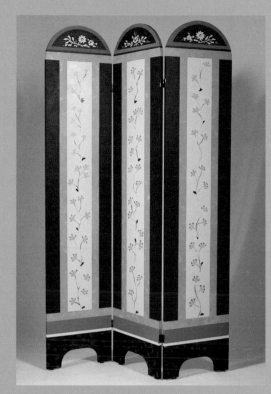

ANNE AUSTIN,
UNTITLED. 2000.
7 X 4 FT. (2.1 X 1.2 M).
WOOD PANELS; ACRYLIC PAINT.
PHOTO BY ARTIST.

BILL KEENAN,
DUALITY SCREEN. 2000.
72 X 78 X 1 IN.
(180 X 195 X 2.5 CM).
SCREEN MADE OF HONDURAN
MAHOGANY, FIDDLEBACK
MAHOGANY VENEER, LACE
WOOD, COLOR CORE, FIBER
PAPER, VARIOUS JOINERY
(DESIGN HAS DIFFERENT
WOOD PANELING AND CON-
STRUCTION ON FRONT AND
BACK). PHOTO BY GREG
ANDERSON.

FAUX FINISH SCREEN

THIS STATELY FOUR-PANEL SCREEN SHOWS OFF FOUR FAUX FINISHES WITHIN THE BOUNDARIES OF A STENCILED ROPE DESIGN. USE THE COLORS AND FINISHES DESCRIBED BELOW, OR ALTER THEM TO SUIT YOUR TASTE.

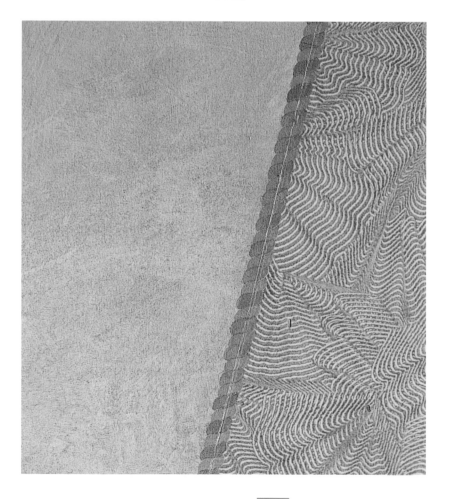

Materials & Tools

2 sheets of ¾-inch (1.9 cm) x 4 x 8-foot (1.2 x 2.4 m) smooth plywood

Sawhorses with large piece of plywood or other large work surface

Jigsaw

C-clamps

Panel template (see fig. 1 on page 34)

Fine- and medium-grit sandpaper

Small handheld sander (optional)

Tack cloth

Drop cloth

Latex primer

Paint trays with several disposable liners

3 paint rollers with ¼-inch (6 mm) nap

1-inch-wide (2.5 cm) flat paintbrush

Semigloss latex interior paint in dark blue-green, golden brown, and antique gold

Long straightedge

Pencil

Artist's low-tack masking tape

Spoon

Water-based clear glaze

4 plastic mixing containers (such as empty yogurt containers, food containers, or small plastic paint buckets)

Instructions

1. On top of your work surface, cut out four identical 18-inch-wide (45.7 cm) wood panels following the panel template for the top cuts (see pages 11 and 12 for detailed instructions about cutting). Cut the panels to a height of your choice—ours measures 5½ feet (1.7 m) at the highest point.

2. Lightly sand the edges, fronts, and backs of each panel. Wipe down the panels with the tack cloth to remove the dust.

3. Spread out the drop cloth on your work surface or floor. Pour the water-based primer into a paint tray, and apply an even coat with one of the ¼-inch (6 mm) nap rollers to the back of each panel. Let it dry. Flip the panels over, and roll a coat of primer on the front of each panel. Prime the sides and edges of the panels with the 1-inch-wide (2.5 cm) paintbrush. When all areas have dried, lightly sand the panels again.

4. Use a clean roller to apply two coats of dark blue-green paint to the backs of each panel, allowing the paint to dry between coats.

5. Use another roller to paint the fronts and sides of the panels with two coats of golden brown paint. Allow the paint to dry.

6. Line up the panels on your work surface, floor, or against a

wall. Beginning on the first panel, use the long straightedge and pencil to mark a diagonal line from the upper right corner down to the bottom of the panel. Draw the same line on the fourth panel. On the second and third panels, mark the diagonals from the top right corner to the bottom left corner of each panel.)

7. Run a strip of masking tape underneath each of the lines. Burnish the tape with a spoon so that paint won't seep under it.

8. Mix one part blue-green paint with three parts glaze in a plastic container. To create a green "rag roll" finish on the top sections and sides of panels one and two, apply the blue-green wash with the sponge roller to the sections. Next, roll up a damp, lint-free rag, place it on the edge of the panel, and roll it in different directions until you've covered all of the blue-green area. Try not to roll over areas twice. Allow the panels to dry while you move on to the other two panels.

9. Make a gold wash by stirring one part golden brown paint with three parts glaze in one of the plastic containers. Use loose strokes and the 4-inch-wide (10.2 cm) paintbrush to paint the gold wash on the

top sections of the third and fourth panels, moving from the top of each panel down to the tape. Paint the adjoining sides as well. Dab the painted surfaces with a bunched up damp rag to soften the appearance of the paint strokes. Allow all four panels to dry completely.

10. Remove the tape from each of the panels. Tape ABOVE the lines this time, protecting the areas that you've just painted.

11. Use the same golden brown mixture you used in step 9 to paint even, vertical strokes with the 3-inch-wide (7.6 cm) paintbrush on the bottom sections and sides of panels one and two.

12. Starting at the top of each newly painted section, hold the wallpaper brush parallel to the screen, and drag it all the way down the panel. Wipe the brush with a rag before making the next adjacent sweep down the panel. Continue until both sections are done. Use the same technique for the sides of the screen, and allow it to dry.

13. Sponge roll the same blue-green wash you used in step 8 on the bottom sections and sides of panels three and four. Place the

MATERIALs & Tools

3 paint-stirring sticks

Damp lint-free rags (available at home supply stores)

2 paint sponge rollers

4-inch-wide (10.2 cm) paintbrush

Lint-free rag (available at home supply stores)

3-inch-wide (7.6 cm) paintbrush

Wallpaper brush

Fine-toothed rubber hair comb

Clear polyester film (available at craft stores)

Fine-tipped black marker

Craft knife

12-inch-square (30.5 cm) sheet of glass or other cutting surface

Stencil adhesive spray

Cosmetic sponges

Small tubes of acrylic paint in gold and antique gold

Paper towels

Acrylic varnish

6 double-acting/butterfly hinges with screws, each hinge measuring ¾ x 1¾ inches (1.9 x 4.4 cm)

Electric drill/screwdriver

teeth of the rubber comb on the surface of the panel, and carve scallops in the glaze until the sections are covered with the pattern. Keep wiping the comb to keep the scallops consistent. Allow the glaze to dry. Remove the tape.

1 4 . On a piece of paper, draw out a pattern for the rope, using the photo on page 32 as a guide. Place the design underneath the film. Use the black marker to trace it onto the polyester film, repeating the pattern to make as long a stencil as you'd like. Position the film on the piece of glass or other hard surface, and cut out the stencil with the craft knife, skipping every other rope shape when you cut.

1 5 . Spray the back of the stencil with stencil adhesive spray, and center it on the top edge of the diagonal line on the first panel.

1 6 . Dip the end of a cosmetic sponge into a small amount of gold acrylic paint. Press the sponge on a paper towel to wipe off any excess paint, then dab the sponge on each rope cutout.

1 7 . Carefully lift off the stencil and reposition it on the diagonal below the area you just painted. Continue to reposition and sponge the stencil until you have complet-

ed the diagonal. Clean the stencil in the sink with hot water and a sponge. Allow the paint to dry.

1 8 . Coat the back of the stencil with stencil adhesive spray, and reposition the rope cutouts between the ones that you painted. Sponge in blank areas of the rope with the antique gold acrylic paint to make a continuous line.

1 9 . Follow steps 15 through 18 to paint the rope designs on the remaining three panels, following the diagonal lines.

2 0 . When completely dry, use a sponge roller to apply a coat of acrylic varnish to the top and sides of the screen. Allow it to dry thoroughly.

2 1 . Hinge the screen (see pages 15 and 16 for instructions).

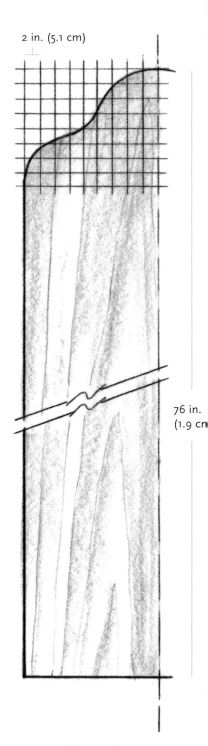

2 in. (5.1 cm)

76 in. (1.9 cm)

Figure 1

Gallery

BARRY R. YAVENER AND JUDY BURKE-BYRNE, *CELTIC IMAGES*. 1999. 68 x 56 x 1¾ IN. (170 x 140 x 4.4 CM). SCREEN CONSTRUCTED OF RED OAK WITH MORTISE AND-TENON JOINERY; HAND PAINTED IMAGES IN ACRYLIC. PHOTO BY TOM LOONAN.

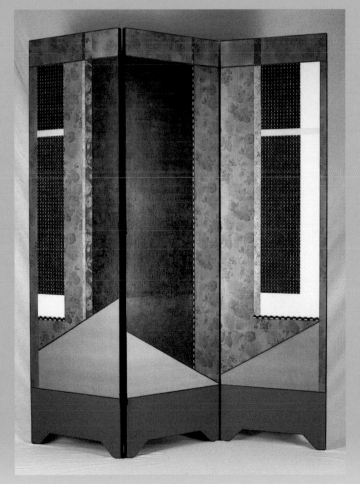

ALLAN MCCULLOCH, *THREE-PANEL SCREEN WITH ABSTRACT INTERIOR*. 2000. 74 x 60 x 1½ IN. (185 x 150 x 3.8 CM). WOOD PANELS; PAINTED, LAMINATED WITH DECORATIVE PAPERS. PHOTO BY ARTIST.

ARTS AND CRAFTS STENCILED FIRE SCREEN

THIS DECORATIVE FIRE SCREEN WITH AN ARTS AND CRAFTS MOTIF CAN BE USED AS A LOVELY COVER FOR YOUR FIREPLACE DURING WARMER MONTHS. IN THE WINTER, YOU CAN USE IT TO DEFLECT HEAT IF PLACED A SAFE DISTANCE AWAY FROM THE FIRE.

Materials & Tools

Salvage wooden fireplace screen or salvage wooden stand made for holding a mirror (You may be able find and use an old screen that is beyond restoration; or, as we did, find an old, empty stand that was probably made to hold a mirror, and have a carpenter cut a curved plywood screen to fit it.)

Liquid detergent (optional)

Scrub brush (optional)

Clean rag (optional)

Medium- and fine-grit sandpaper

Small handheld sander (optional)

3-inch (7.6 cm) flat paintbrush

Semigloss latex paint in dark color

Border stencil with arts and craft motif (available at home supply and craft supply stores)

Stencil adhesive spray

Medium-sized stencil brush

Stencil paint in light color that complements dark background color (available at craft supply stores)

Clear latex varnish

Instructions

1. If you're using an old screen, remove any dirt or loose paint from the screen and stand with the brush and soapy water. Wipe it dry with a clean rag.

2. Sand the surface of the screen and the stand as needed to smooth it.

3. Paint the screen and stand with two coats of the dark latex paint. Allow the paint to dry thoroughly.

4. Coat the back of the stencil with stencil adhesive spray. Position it on the front of the screen at the top, making sure that it is level.

5. Dip the stencil brush in the stencil paint (the brush should be dry), and daub off any excess paint. Hold the brush perpendicular to the surface of the screen, and pounce up and down within the contours of the stencil to create a drybrush effect. Apply more pigment around the edges of the stencil to create darker areas. Lift one corner of the stencil to check for coverage, and reapply paint as needed until you like the effect.

6. After 48 hours of drying time, use the flat paintbrush to apply two coats of clear varnish to the screen and stand.

Gallery

Edward Pelton and Dale Morse,
Clay Hill Forge, #1 Firescreen. 2000.
40 x 36 x 2 in. (100 x 90 x 5 cm).
Reforged mild steel flat bar assembled with
copper rivets; double fireplace with a
matching screen covering both openings.
Photo by John Williamson.

Elizabeth Brim,
Snakes in the Grass. 1997.
41 x 43 x 8½ in.
(103 x 108 x 21.6 cm).
Forged snakes; forged welded
grass; faux finish grass and
frame finished with shoe pol-
ish and yellow ochre iron
oxide. Photo by Tom Mills.

DESIGNER: KATHERINE AIMONE

EMBOSSED VELVET SCREEN

THIS SHIMMERING VELVET SCREEN IS EASY TO MAKE. ALTHOUGH EMBOSSING THE VELVET WITH STAMPS TAKES SOME TIME, THE RESULTS ARE EXTREMELY IMPRESSIVE. SEWING THE PANELS IS A TASK THAT EVEN A BEGINNER CAN UNDERTAKE.

Materials & Tools

Unassembled wooden frame screen with dowels for holding fabric or paper (our screen has three openings that measure 12 x 52½ inches [30.5 cm x 1.3 m] each with dowels set in 1 inch [2.5 cm] from the top and bottom of each opening) *

Drop cloth

Latex primer

2 paintbrushes, each 2 to 3 inches (5 to 7.6 cm) wide

Semigloss latex paint in color of your choice for frame

Semigloss latex house paint in slightly darker color than main color (optional)

6 yards (5.4 m) of 45-inch-wide (1.14 m) rayon/acetate velvet for the front and back of the panels (If your frame is sized differently from ours, add 1½ inches [3.8 cm] to the length of the frame opening and 10 inches [25.4 cm] to the width of the opening to determine the panel size. Double the amount of fabric to account for both front and back panels.)

*THE TRADITIONAL CHANGING SCREEN THAT WE USED CAN BE ORDERED FROM WALNUT HOLLOW WOODCRAFTS, 1409 STATE ROAD 23, DODGEVILLE, WISCONSIN, 53533-2112; PHONE: (608) 935-2341, FAX: (608) 935-3029

CONTINUED ON NEXT PAGE

Instructions

1 . Assemble the wooden screen according to the manufacturer's instructions, leaving the dowels to be inserted later.

2 . Place the drop cloth on the floor of your work space, and paint the screen with a coat of wood primer. Allow it to dry.

3 . Next, paint the screen with the colored, semigloss paint. Allow the screen to dry completely. Wash the brush thoroughly, and allow it to dry.

4 . If you wish to create an antique effect, apply a small amount of the contrasting paint to the end of the other brush. With a quick motion, flick the end of the dry brush on the painted surface, allowing the brushstrokes to show. Add contrasting accents with the paint until you achieve the effect that you want. Allow the screen to dry, and set it aside.

5 . Cut the velvet in half so that you can use one section for the front of the panels.

6 . To emboss the velvet, place the rubber stamp(s) faceup on the surface of your ironing board.

Drape the velvet on top of it, nap-side-down. Set the iron to medium setting.

7 . Spritz the velvet with a light misting of water (do not saturate the velvet). Place the iron flat and directly on top of the stamp. Hold it in place for about 20 seconds. Remove the iron, and check the impression of the stamp. (If the impression is clear, you've timed it properly. If not, hold the iron down longer the next time.)

8 . Move the velvet over slightly so that it is in position for its next impression. Spritz and iron as you did before. Continue this process across the surface of the velvet to make a pattern, keeping in mind that the impressions need not be perfectly spaced or precisely the same (for instance, partial impressions make an interesting punctuation point in the design).

9 . Cut out three identical panels from both the embossed velvet and the backing velvet that measure 54 x 22 inches (1.4 m x 55.9 cm) each (or a panel size to fit your frame).

10. On the long edges of the panels, mark 2½ inches (6.4 cm) from each end, and stitch front to

back (right sides of velvet and backing together) between the marks shown in figure 1, using a ½-inch (1.3 cm) seam allowance.

1 1. Stitch across the top end of each panel using a ½-inch (1.3 cm) seam allowance. Stitch across the bottom end, leaving a 7-inch (17.8 cm) gap in the center for turning the panel.

1 2. Turn the panels right side out, and press around the edges lightly on a low setting from the BACK side, keeping the seam allowances tucked in where the stitching stops. (Take care not to press too hard, or you may disturb the embossed prints.) Slip stitch the opening at the bottom closed.

Figure 1

1 3. To create the casings on each panel, stitch across the top and bottom 1 inch (2.5 cm) from the edges, and again 2 inches (5 cm) from the edges (see figure 2). This provides you with a 1-inch-wide (2.5 cm) ruffle and casing at the ends of each panel.

1 4. Once the sewing is complete, slide each of the top dowels into one of the sleeves on each panel, and gather the fabric to fit (see figure 2). Slide each dowel carefully into the holes provided for holding it at the top of each frame.

1 5. Slide the bottom dowels into the bottom sleeves, gather, and pull the fabric slightly while you insert each into the holes at the bottom. (If you have trouble getting the dowels inserted, they may be a bit too long. You can trim them with a straight saw if needed.)

1 6. Hinge the screen (see pages 15 and 16 for instructions).

MATERIALS & TOOLS

Ironing board

Rubber stamp(s) of your choice with broad lines

Spray bottle with mist setting filled with water

Clothes iron

Sewing machine and thread that matches velvet

Straight pins

Sewing needle

6 double-acting/butterfly hinges and screws (hardware should accompany manufactured screen)

Electric drill/screwdriver

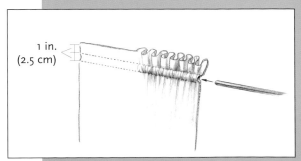

1 in.
(2.5 cm)

Figure 2

DESIGNER: RICKIE R. WESBROOKS

MADISON AVENUE UPHOLSTERED SCREEN

THIS DESIGNER WANTED TO SHOW OFF AND PRESERVE A BOLT OF UPHOLSTERY FABRIC THAT HE DESIGNED, SO HE USED FRAME PANELS AS THE SUBSTRATE FOR STRETCHING THE HEAVY-WEIGHT FABRIC. THIS STATELY SCREEN STANDS 7 FEET (2 M) TALL—MADE FOR A HOUSE OR APARTMENT WITH TALL CEILINGS—BUT YOU CAN ADJUST THE HEIGHT TO FIT YOUR TASTE AND NEEDS.

Materials & Tools

11 pieces of 1 x 1½-inch (2.5 x 3.8 cm) hardwood such as mahogany or oak, each 8 feet long (2.4 m)

Sawhorses and large piece of plywood or other large work surface

Framer's square

Measuring tape

Miter box with saw

Pattern for feet (see fig. 1, next page)

1 x 2-inch (2.5 x 5 cm) pieces of hardwood (we used mahogany) cut into eight 4-inch-long (10.2 cm) pieces

Jigsaw

Electric drill/screwdriver

Wood stain of your choice and paintbrush (optional)

3 grades of sandpaper, from coarse to fine

Tack cloth

High-grade brush for water-based sealants

Water-based polyurethane

Fabric scissors

6 yards (5.4 m) of 8-foot-wide (2.4 m) polyester batting (low loft)

Staple gun

¼-inch (6 mm) staples (rustproof, if available)

Tack hammer

10 yards (9 m) of 1 x 32-inch (2.5 x 81.3 cm) polyester batting

Sewing needle with hole large enough to accommodate thread

CONTINUED ON NEXT PAGE

Instructions

1. Before building the frame, make sure that each piece of wood you choose has straight edges.

2. Place each piece of wood on your work surface (such as a couple of sawhorses with a large piece of plywood on top). Use the framer's square to check one end of the wood to make sure it is square. Use the measuring tape and the framer's square to mark off eight pieces of the wood with an 84-inch (2.1 m) length or shorter length of your choice (these pieces will determine the height of your screen). Set aside the remaining three pieces.

3. Place each length of wood in the miter box set at a 90° angle, and carefully align the saw with the cutting mark before sawing off the excess wood on each piece. You've now cut the sides for the four frames.

4. To cut eight crossbars (the pieces at the top and bottom of the frame) and four crosspieces (the pieces in the center of the frame) that measure 21 inches (53.3 cm) each, mark off four lengths on each of the remaining three boards. Follow the same procedure for cutting as you did to cut the longer pieces.

5. Assemble each frame with the technique shown on pages 13 to 15. Add each of the crossbar supports to the center of each frame. Use the framer's square as needed to check the angles.

6. Trace the cutting pattern for the feet onto each of the eight 1 x 2-inch (2.5 x 5 cm) hardwood pieces. Use the jigsaw to cut the pattern out of each block. (Make all straight cuts first, followed by curves.)

7. On the bottom of each foot, make two marks ⅞ inch (2.2 cm) from each edge on the long axis and centered at ½ inch (1.3 cm). Use a 3/16-inch (5 mm) drill bit to drill the holes from the bottom to the top.

8. Use a ⅜-inch (9.5 mm) or slightly larger drill bit to drill a hole approximately 1¼ inches deep (3.2 cm) in the original hole. (This hole will allow you to place a screwdriver into the block to recess the screw into the frame.)

9. Apply the wood stain to the feet with the paintbrush. Allow the feet to dry.

10. To prepare the frame for upholstering, we took an extra step

to insure long life for the fabric. (If you are creating a piece with expensive fabric, we suggest that you undertake this step.) To begin, sand each of the frames with the coarsest to the finest sandpaper to create very smooth surfaces. Remove the dust with a tack cloth. Use the high-grade brush to apply a coat of water-based polyurethane to all of the frame surfaces, and allow it to dry completely.

11. Next, you'll begin the upholstery process (see pages 17 to 19 for illustrated information). Place one of the frames on your work surface, and use scissors to cut out a piece of the low-loft batting that is slightly larger than the frame. Lay the batting over the frame, and center it.

12. Staple the batting to the front, placing the staples at diagonals, beginning at the center crossbar. Space the staples at least 2 inches (5 cm) apart. Use the tack hammer as needed to secure the staples.

13. Move to the center of the top of the frame, and staple the batting, stretching it lightly. Staple the batting to the other two centers of the remaining side and bottom of the frame.

14. After you've stapled the batting in the center portions of each side of the frame, work your way around the frame to staple the remaining edges in place. Use scissors to trim away the excess.

15. Turn the frame over. From the 1-inch-wide (2.5 cm) batting, cut two pieces that fit inside the two open spaces of the frame. Press them into place so that they fill the frame and lie smooth and flat.

16. Staple low-loft batting to the other side of the frame as you did in steps 11 through 14.

17. Stand one of the frames in an open doorway, or upright on its side on your worktable. Thread the sewing needle with a 3-yard (2.7 m) length of the black thread. Beginning in one of the corners of the frame, use long stitches to sew a very large "X" through the layers of batting to hold them in place. Secure the ends of the thread with knots, and cut off the excess thread. (Remember that these threads won't show; they're only there to prevent the batting from sagging or shifting later on.)

18. Repeat steps 13 through 17 to secure batting to the remaining three frames.

MATERIALS & TOOLS

1 spool of black heavy-duty thread

10 yards (9 m) of 54-inch-wide (1.4 m) upholstery fabric

Pushpins

12 double-acting/butterfly hinges with screws, each hinge measuring ¾ x 1¾ inches (1.9 x 4.4 cm)

22 yards (19.8 m) of ⅞-inch (2.2 cm) trim in color that matches your fabric

PVA acid-free glue made for paper or fabric

⅝-inch (1.6 cm) flat artist's paintbrush

Stepladder

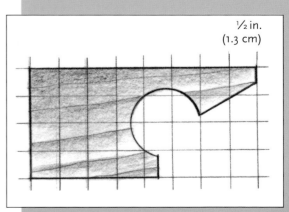

½ in. (1.3 cm)

Figure 1

19. Lay the fabric facedown on your work surface. Fold the fabric in half along the width, and cut it in half along the fold so that you have two long pieces of the same size (each 27 inches [68.6 cm] wide).

20. Place one of the frames along the length of one of the long pieces, and hold the fabric in place temporarily with pushpins to check the orientation of the fabric if you're using a patterned cloth. Remove the pins, and cut out a fabric panel that is the length of the frame plus 4 inches (10.2 cm). (The width remains the same.) Cut out seven more panels that are the same size as the first panel.

21. You are now ready to staple the fabric to the frame. Place one of the panels facedown on your work surface with a frame on top of it. Beginning at the top of your fabric, stretch it over the side of the frame, and staple once in the CENTER of the length close to THE FAR EDGE of the width (so that you'll be able to easily place the hinges in the center later without hitting staples).

22. Move to the bottom of the panel, and add another staple in the center of the panel. Lightly pull the fabric to each side of the staples, and staple it into place. Working from the center out, continue to staple, and fold the fabric under at the corner to hide it. Repeat this process to staple the fabric to the sides, lining up your staples along the other far edges of the sides of each panel so that the center is left free for hinging.

23. Flip the frame over, and attach another fabric panel to the other side, keeping the orientation of the fabric in mind so that it works with the front.

24. Repeat steps 20 through 23 to upholster the remaining three panels.

25. Use the instructions on pages 15 and 16 to assist you in attaching the hinges to the panels. You'll attach the frames with three sets of four hinges where the panels join, alternating the hinging from one side to the other to create an accordion-style configuration when you're finished. On each joining edge, place the outermost hinges 6 inches (15.2 cm) from the top and the bottom of the frame. Between these hinges, space two more hinges 24 inches (61 cm) apart.

26. Once you've hinged the screen, set it upright so that you can attach the trim. You'll need a stepladder to reach the top.

27. Measure from the lower edge of the outermost panel across the top and down to the first hinge, and add about 2 inches (5 cm) to this measurement. Cut a piece of trim this length.

28. Use the artist's brush to apply glue to the edge of the screen in sections as you slowly work the trim onto the screen. Use a pushpin to hold the trim in place after you glue it, then move on to the next section, adding trim between the hinges. Continue this process until the trim is in place.

29. Repeat steps 27 and 28 on the opposite outermost panel.

30. For the remaining sides of the panels, follow the same procedure for measuring, cutting, gluing, and tacking pieces of trim to fit the sides of the frames between the hinges. Allow the glue to dry, and remove the pins.

Gallery

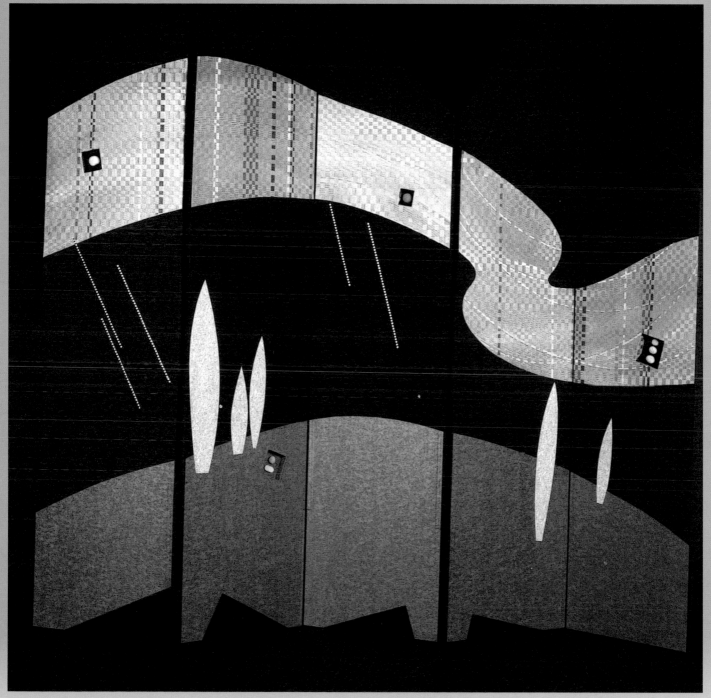

JoAnne Schiavone, *Weaving Your Way Home II.* 2001. 6 ft. x 90 x ¾ in. (1.8 m x 225 x 1.9 cm). Five panel folding screen; woven paste paper, handmade papers, fabric, wood, stones. Photo by Karen Mauch.

DESIGNER: KATHERINE AIMONE

STAMPED AND EMBOSSED PAPER INLAY SCREEN

U SE STAMPS AND EMBOSSING POWDERS ON HANDMADE PAPERS TO CREATE BEAUTIFUL INSETS THAT TRANSFORM A TRADITIONAL JAPANESE WOOD AND PAPER SCREEN INTO A UNIQUE PIECE. THIS SCREEN IS AN EXERCISE IN VISUAL COMPOSITION WITHIN A GRID SYSTEM.

Materials & Tools

Japanese-style lattice screen with paper/polyester backing (available at some furniture stores)

Ruler

Piece of heavy paper or poster board

Medium to heavyweight handmade white or off-white paper (available through art supply stores)

Scissors

Leaf or floral stamps of your choice that fit comfortably into openings created by lattice of screen

Transparent embossing ink pad

Embossing powders in colors of your choice (we used red, yellow, black, gold, and silver)

Wax paper

Embossing heat tool

Low-tack artist's tape

2 or 3 sheets of handmade paper in solid accent colors

Soft pencil

Craft knife

PVA archival glue made for paper

INSTRUCTIONS

1 . From the back of the screen, use the ruler to measure the width and length of one of the openings in the lattice, adding ½ inch (1.3 cm) to each measurement. Use these measurements to cut out a piece of heavy paper or poster board to use as a template.

2 . Look at your screen and decide approximately how many paper inlays you want to use to decorate it. (This number need not be exact.) Repeatedly trace the template onto the white or off-white handmade paper, and cut out the pieces.

3 . On the handmade papers, use embossing inks to stamp images of

your choice, and sprinkle them with embossing powders. After sprinkling, tap the powders lightly off of each image onto a swatch of wax paper. Bend the paper slightly, and pour the excess powders back into their jars. (Keep in mind that you can emboss a stamped image with several embossing powders, a section at a time, for interesting effects.)

4 . Use the embossing tool to melt the powders after you've applied them. Move the tool back and forth over each image, and watch carefully until the powder is transformed into a shiny surface.

5 . After you've created a number of inlay papers, decide where you want to place them by taping them temporarily on the front of the screen with low-tack artist's tape. Move back from the screen, and look at the overall configuration and how the inlays relate to one another. Move them around, and try out different juxtapositions.

6 . As punctuation points in the design, stamp and emboss a few of the solid-colored papers, but add only a few, since your eye will immediately be drawn to the solid-colored areas.

edge of the front of the paper inlay, and smear it. (The glue will dry clear, so don't worry about speading it too much.)

1 O. Place the paper inlay facedown on the back of the screen over the opening. Use your fingers to lightly rub back and forth on the

edges of the paper so that it adheres and the paper begins to bond.

1 1. Repeat steps 8 through 10 to add the remaining paper inlays. Allow the papers to dry in a safe area (away from curious cats!) for several hours.

7. Once you've decided on placement of the paper inlays, remove each and use the soft pencil to write a small number on the back. Write a corresponding number directly on the white panel behind it. This will provide you with a map for placing the pieces.

8. Once all the papers are removed, lay the screen facedown on the floor or on a large table.

9. Use the craft knife to carefully cut out one of the panels, sliding the edge of the knife against the sides of the lattice strips as you go. Find the paper inlay that matches the number on the panel. Squeeze a thin line of archival paper glue around the edge of the opening in the frame, and smear it slightly with the tip of the bottle. Squeeze another line of glue around the

ALTERNATIVE IDEA: USE SOLID-COLORED PAPERS AND THE SAME TECHNIQUE TO MAKE A MONDRIAN-INSPIRED SCREEN.

DESIGNER: MIKE CALLAHAN

FREESTANDING DIVIDER WALL

THIS VERSATILE ROOM DIVIDER IS ESSENTIALLY A MOVABLE WALL ON WHEELS. IT CAN BE BUILT OUT OF CONSTRUCTION-GRADE WOOD AND DRYWALL WITH BASIC TOOLS AND A KNOWLEDGE OF CARPENTRY. IF YOU DON'T HAVE THE EXPERIENCE OR TOOLS TO BUILD IT YOURSELF, HIRE A CARPENTER TO BUILD IT, USING THE ILLUSTRATION AND INSTRUCTIONS PROVIDED. YOU CAN ADJUST THE DIMENSIONS AS YOU WISH. (THE FOLLOWING DIRECTIONS ARE FOR A DIVIDER THAT IS 78 INCHES [1.9 M] HIGH, 8 FEET [2 M] WIDE, AND 17 INCHES [43.2 CM] DEEP.)

Materials & Tools

17 2 x 4 construction-grade studs, each 8-feet (2.4 m) in length

Measuring tape

Long metal straightedge

Sawhorses and large piece of plywood or other work surface

C-clamps

Circular saw

Box 16-penny (16d) nails

Hammer

Carpenter's square

Wood glue

Jigsaw

¾-inch (1.9 cm) x 4 x 8-foot (1.2 x 2.4 m) sheet of AC grade plywood

Box of 8-penny (8d) finishing nails, 1½-inches (3.8 cm) long

4 locking, non-swiveling casters, each 4 inches (10.2 cm) in diameter

Electric screwdriver

5 sheets of 4 x 8-foot (1.2 x 2.4 m) drywall

Box of drywall nails

Utility knife

Tin snips

4 drywall corner beads, 8 feet long (2.4 m) each

Roll of drywall tape

Drywall knife

1 gallon (3.8 L) of drywall joint compound

Small electric sander

Paint or wallpaper of your choice for finishing

Instructions

1 . Use figure 1 on page 57 to guide you through the following steps. You'll begin construction by building two separate frames that measure 80 inches (2 m) long by 72½ inches (1.8 m) high from the 2 x 4 studs. To do this, mark off and cut four 2 x 4s to 81-inch (2 m) lengths with the circular saw (these will serve as your horizontal plates). Cut twelve 2 x 4s that are 69½ inches (1.7 m) long (these will serve as your vertical studs).

2 . Lay out the horizontal pieces for each frame on the floor or your work surface with six vertical 2 x 4s spaced on 16-inch (40.6 cm) centers between each. (This spacing will allow you to use a standard sheet of drywall without cutting it.)

3 . Drive 16d nails through the horizontal plates to hold the vertical studs in place. You should now have two identical walls. Check for the squareness of your walls with the carpenter's square and by measuring from corner to corner diagonally to make sure that the dimensions are identical. If not, adjust by racking the unit.

4 . Next, cut four 16-inch (40.6 cm) pieces of 2 x 4 to be used as spac-

ers. Using a scrap piece of 2 x 4 as a guide, notch the pieces with the jigsaw to facilitate assembly. (See the illustration for clarification.)

5 . With the help of a friend, stand the two walls upright and use 16d nails to attach a spacer at each corner. Cut four filler pieces to fit between the studs and against the spacers. Nail the fillers to the spacers with 16d nails. (The filler pieces will support the drywall later.)

6 . Using the finished outside dimensions of the top and bottom of your divider, cut two pieces of ¾-inch (1.9 cm) plywood to size. Sandwich the walls between the top and bottom plywood pieces, and check the squareness of the assembly with a carpenter's square before assembling it with wood glue and 8d nails.

7 . Position the wheels at the four corners of the bottom of the assembly close to the outside edges to ensure stability. Screw them into place with the hardware provided.

8 . To cover your divider with drywall, measure the width and length of the assembly, and cut the drywall to fit. It is important to cut your widths so that one factory edge falls at the middle of a stud. This

will allow you to fasten adjoining pieces to the same stud. (Note that the 8-foot-long [2.4 m] factory edge of a sheet of drywall is slightly tapered to allow for smooth taping.)

9. To cut the drywall, use a straightedge and utility knife to score through the paper covering so that you can break the sheet along the score before cutting the backing paper. Nail the drywall to the studs with the drywall nails, making sure to set the heads deep enough so they can be covered with drywall compound when finishing.

10. Use the tin snips to cut the corner beads to length, and attach them with drywall nails to cover the length of all eight corners.

11. Apply drywall tape to all of your seams before applying several coats of joint compound with the drywall knife, sanding between coats. (If you are not familiar with drywall finishing techniques, pick up simple instructions from your home building supplier.)

12. Finish your divider with paint or wallpaper of your choice. After it dries and you are ready to move it, roll it carefully to avoid tipping it over.

Figure 1

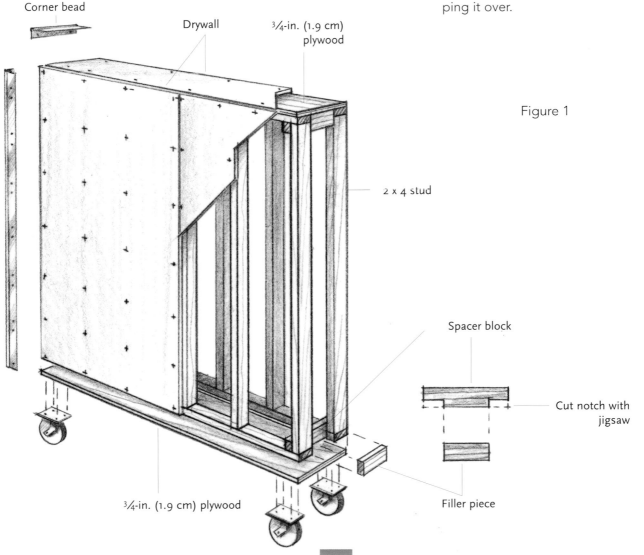

Corner bead

Drywall

3/4-in. (1.9 cm) plywood

2 x 4 stud

Spacer block

Cut notch with jigsaw

3/4-in. (1.9 cm) plywood

Filler piece

RECYCLED
AND ALTERED

IN THE PAST, WHO WOULD'VE DREAMED THAT TODAY WE'D RELISH RUMMAG-
ING THROUGH PILES OF DISCARDED CEILING TILES OR CORRUGATED METAL?
OR THAT WE'D SPEND OUR SATURDAY AFTERNOONS SCAVENGING THRIFT STORES
TO FIND OLD MAGAZINES TO MAKE INTO STYLISH COLLAGES? YESTERDAY'S JUNK
PILE IS DEFINITELY TODAY'S TREASURE HOUSE! THIS SECTION SHOWS YOU EXCIT-
ING WAYS TO RECYCLE MATERIALS INTO SCREENS FILLED WITH CHARACTER.

DESIGNER: LORIN KNOUSE

RECYCLED DOOR SCREEN

THE DOORS USED TO COMPOSE THIS SCREEN WERE UNEARTHED BY THE DESIGNER FROM THE BASEMENT OF AN OLD BANK BUILDING. THEY WERE GIVEN NEW LIFE AS A STRIKING, FUNCTIONAL ROOM DIVIDER.

Materials & Tools

3 salvage/reclaimed doors

Sawhorses

Liquid detergent

Scrubbing brush

Stripping solvent (optional)

4-inch-wide (10.2 cm) paintbrush

Semigloss interior latex paint in three colors of your choice

80-grit sandpaper

Hand rasp

Protective gloves

2½-inch (6.4 cm) sash brush

Dark wood stain

Clean cotton rags

Paste wax

100-grit sandpaper

Clear gloss polyurethane spray

Door numbers, letters, or signs of your choice

4 large door hinges, each 4 inches (10.2 cm) long, with screws

Black enamel spray paint

Electric drill/screwdriver

Window cleaner (optional)

Instructions

1 . Place the sawhorses outside near a water hose. Balance each door on the sawhorses while you scrub it thoroughly with detergent and water to remove any dirt or loose paint.

2 . Remove any hardware from the doors. If the hardware is covered with old paint, use stripping solvent to remove the paint.

3 . Place each door, one at a time, on the sawhorses, and use the 4-inch (10.2 cm) brush to paint the front of each of the doors with a different color of paint. After the paint has dried, flip each of the doors over and paint the other side with the same color.

4 . To create a distressed/aged look, use 80-grit sandpaper to sand all of the outside edges of the doors to expose bare wood through the paint on each door. Choose areas of the doors that might be worn naturally through use, and further distress them by rubbing the hand rasp on those areas to reveal old paint colors beneath the new.

5 . Put on protective gloves, and use the sash brush to apply wood stain to the wood surfaces of the doors, making sure to blend in any obvious brushstrokes. Let the stain stand for up to an hour for a darker finish. Use a rag to wipe away any stain that runs.

6 . After the stain stands, gently wipe away any remaining wet stain on the surfaces. (Leave more stain in corners where shadows might fall on the piece.)

7 . Allow the stain to cure for 24 to 36 hours. When dry, use a cotton rag to apply a thin coat of paste wax to the doors. Buff the wax with another clean rag to a low luster.

8. Gently sand the surfaces of the metal pieces with 100-grit sandpaper to reveal the bare metal on the outside edges and corners.

9. Lay out the hardware, and apply two thin coats of polyurethane spray to the pieces. When dry, reinstall the hardware on the doors.

10. Add letters, numbers, or signs of your choice to the doors. (Use the accompanying hardware, or glue them to the doors.)

11. Spray paint the 4-inch (10.2 cm) connecting hinges with black enamel spray paint. When dry, attach them to the doors with the electric screwdriver, making sure that they are aligned properly.

12. If your doors have any windows, clean them with window cleaner.

ALTERNATIVE IDEA: DESIGNER DOUGLAS MADARAS USED OLD SHUTTERS FROM WHICH HE REMOVED THE TOP PANELS AND REPLACED THEM WITH GLASS BEFORE DISTRESSING THE SURFACES WITH PAINT AND SANDING.

CORRUGATED METAL SCREEN

INSPIRED BY THE FASCINATING IMPER-FECTIONS OF OLD ROOF TIN FOUND AT THE BOTTOM OF A PILE IN A SALVAGE YARD, THIS DESIGNER CAME UP WITH A UNIQUE WAY OF USING IT TO MAKE A SCREEN THAT HIDES A STORAGE CORNER IN HIS OFFICE.

Materials & Tools

*3 sheets of old, corrugated galva-
nized roof tin (look for abraded
and distressed pieces available at
salvage yards)*

Safety glasses

Heavy work gloves

*Work surface such as sawhorses with
large piece of plywood on top*

*Circular saw fitted with 7-inch
(17.8 cm) corundum abrasive blade*

C-clamps

Heavy hammer (at least 20 ounces)

Clean rag

*Small can of red mahogany wood
stain*

*6 pieces of ¾ x 4-inch-wide (1.9 x
10.2 cm) grooved casing/base molding, each cut to the height of your
screen*

*6 pieces of ¼ x ¾-inch (6 mm x
1.9 cm) edge molding, each cut to
the height of your screen (to use for
framing on the back)*

*6 pieces ¼ x ¾-inch (6 mm x
1.9 cm) edge molding, cut to ½
inch (1.3 cm) less than the width of
each panel, to use as crosspieces*

Electric drill/screwdriver

*Box of 1-inch-long (2.5 cm)
anodized black wood screws*

Box of metal finishing washers

Spray acrylic gloss enamel in black

4 large door hinges

Instructions

1 . Put on safety glasses and work gloves. On your work surface, use a 7-inch (17.8 cm) circular saw with a corundum abrasive blade to cut the tin into three identical panels to fit the dimensions of the screen you want to make. (Hold the tin pieces in place with C-clamps as needed.)

2 . Place the tin pieces on a drive-way or other hard, flat surface. Use the heavy hammer to bend or flatten 4 inches (10.2 cm) of the tin on all of the horizontal edges to accommodate the front molding for each panel.

3 . Use a rag to apply red mahogany stain to the fronts and sides of all of the pieces of mold-ing. Allow it to dry.

4 . Place one of the pieces of tin facedown on your work surface. Sandwich the flattened vertical edges of the tin between the ¾ x 4-inch (1.9 x 10.2 cm) molding and the back edge molding. Use C-clamps to hold the assembly in place (see figure 1 on page 67 for guidance).

5 . Use the electric drill fitted with an appropriate bit to make holes down the center of the molding strips, spacing them about 12 inches (30.5 cm) apart. (Drill the holes through the back molding, tin, and about ½-inch [1.3 cm] into the front molding. Do not drill all the way through to the front.)

6 . Slip finishing washers onto each of the black wood screws, and screw the molding and tin together.

7 . Repeat steps 4 through 6 for the remaining two panels.

8 . On the back of the panel that you want to use as your central panel, place one of the crosspieces about a quarter of the way down the back, overlapping the vertical molding strips. Clamp the cross-piece in place, and drill a hole near each end into the molding beneath it. Use washers and screws to attach the crosspiece to the molding. Use the same process to add another crosspiece about the same distance from the bottom of the panel.

9 . On the remaining two panels, add two crosspieces on each, spac-ing them below the crosspieces of the central panel (this will allow you to fold the screen back without the crosspieces touching each other). Attach the crosspieces with screws.

10. Spray the hinges with two coats of black enamel paint, and allow them to dry.

11. Hinge the panels together from the back, so that they do not show when you open out the piece. To do this, place the central panel facedown next to one of the side panels, about ¾ inches (1.9 cm) apart. Screw one of the hinges to the back along the vertical molding just above the crosspiece on the central panel. Screw another hinge at the bottom, below the lower crosspiece on the central panel.

12. Repeat step 11 to hinge the remaining side panel to the other side of the central panel.

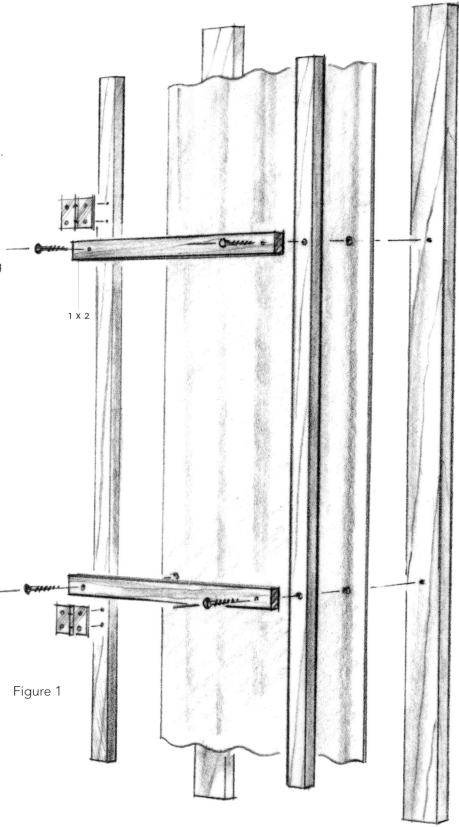

1 X 2

Figure 1

DESIGNER: DIANA LIGHT

GEOMETRIC PLAY SCREEN

SEVERAL HOLLOW-CORE DOORS LEFT OVER FROM A BUILDING PROJECT ARE TRANSFORMED INTO A STRIKING SCREEN DISPLAYING GEOMETRIC DESIGNS THAT ARE REPEATED BUT ALTERED THROUGH CHANGES IN COLOR RELATIONSHIPS.

Materials & Tools

4 hollow-core doors, each 18 inches (45.7 cm) wide

Drop cloth

2 paint rollers

Paint tray with disposable liners

Latex primer

Light purple satin interior latex paint

1-inch-wide (2.5 cm) paintbrush

Carbon paper

Design template (fig. 1)

Artist's low-tack masking tape

Straightedge

Ballpoint pen

Spoon

Artist's acrylic paints in dark purple, olive green, and khaki

Medium-sized artist's paintbrush

Small fan (optional)

6 double-acting/butterfly hinges with screws, each hinge measuring ¾ x 1¾ inches (1.9 x 4.4 cm)

Electric drill/screwdriver

Instructions

1. Cover your work surface or floor with the drop cloth. Use one of the paint rollers to apply a coat of primer to all sides of the doors. Allow the primer to dry.

2. With a clean roller, apply a coat of light purple paint to both sides of the doors. Use the 1-inch-wide (2.5 cm) paintbrush to paint the sides and corners of the doors. Allow the paint to dry thoroughly.

3. Center the carbon paper face-down with the template on top of it, 8 inches (20.3 cm) from the top of one of the doors. Tape both in place with masking tape. Use the straightedge to help you trace the lines of the design with the ballpoint pen. Check periodically to see that the lines have been transferred. Repeat for each of the remaining doors.

4. Tape the lines of the innermost section of the design. Burnish the tape with a spoon so that paint won't seep under it.

5. Select one of the acrylic paints to use, and paint carefully inside the lines. Allow the paint to dry so that you can remove the tape without smearing it. (You can blow air on the work with a small fan to help speed up this process.)

6. Continue to mask off the remaining areas of the design with tape, and paint in the other colors, juxtaposing different colors. (Besides the artist's acrylic paints, you can use the latex paint that you used as your main color as one of the interior colors in the designs. You can also mix a bit of primer with this color to create a slightly lighter shade.)

7. Paint the designs on the remaining three doors, varying the arrangement of the colors. After you're finished, allow the doors to dry overnight.

8. Hinge the screen (see pages 15 and 16 for instructions).

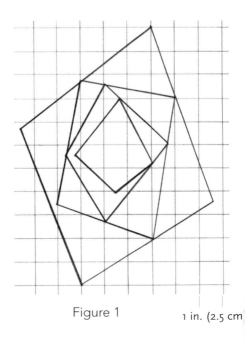

Figure 1   1 in. (2.5 cm

Gallery

LOREN KNOUSE, *RECYCLED WINDOW SCREEN.* 2002, 7 x 4 FT. (2 x 1.2 M), OLD SALVAGED WINDOW, WOOD CONSTRUCTION, LAYERED LATEX PAINTS. PHOTO BY SANDRA STAMBAUGH.

PRESSED TIN
SCREEN

THE TIN FOR THIS STRIKING SCREEN WAS SALVAGED FROM A SCHOOL THAT WAS BEING DEMOLISHED. FOR A CONSISTENT LOOK, TRY TO LOCATE TIN THAT HAS BEEN SALVAGED FROM ONE LOCATION. THE SIZE OF THE SHEETS WILL DETERMINE HOW BIG YOU CAN MAKE YOUR SCREEN.

Materials & Tools

Pressed tin sheets (large enough to fill the front and back of the panels of your frame; see instructions for guidance)

Tin snips

Workbench (such as a long piece of plywood on two sawhorses)

Hammer

Block of scrap wood

Salvaged barn wood or other wood stock (2 x 2s [1½ x 1½-inch (3.8 x 3.9 cm) boards] were used for this project)

Measuring tape

Table saw with dado blade (or handsaw and chisel)

Miter box and saw

Wood glue

C-clamps

Carpenter's square

10-penny (10 d) finishing nails

4 double-acting/butterfly hinges with screws, each hinge measuring ¾ x 1 ¾ inches (1.9 x 4.4 cm)

Instructions

1. Use the tin snips to cut the tin sheets to the size that you intend for your finished screen panels, minus about 1½ inches (3.8 cm) on each side to accomodate the structural frame. Cut two identical sheets for each panel (front and back).

2. Place each tin panel on the floor on your work surface with the block of wood underneath the edges, and hammer the edges flat all the way around.

3. Lay out the panels on the floor as you intend to assemble them back-to-back inside the frames, and measure them to make sure that they're all the same size after hammering. If needed, cut and adjust the edges so that they're straight and of the same dimensions.

4. On your workbench, use the miter box to cut eight boards at 90° that measure the width of the sheets minus ½ inch (1.3 cm). Cut eight more boards that measure the height of the panels plus 1 inch (2.5 cm). (You've now cut the top and bottom rails and the side rails.)

5. Using the dado blade on the table saw, cut a ³⁄₁₆-inch (5 mm) groove down the center of the inside edge of each rail (on one edge only). The groove should be

¼-inch (6 mm) deep. If you don't have a table saw, use a handsaw to cut the grooves, and chisel out the wood carefully.

6. Position the top and bottom rails between the long rails on your work surface at right angles to one another. Leave ½ inch (1.3 cm) between the top and bottom of each side rail and the edges of the shorter rails (see the finished photo for guidance).

7. Glue the two long side rails of the frame to the top rail, and clamp them into place. Use the carpenter's square to check the corners, then allow the glue to dry. Drive finishing nails into the corners to secure them further.

8. Repeat steps 3 through 7 to assemble the top and sides of the remaining frames.

9. Position two of the tin sheets back to back, and slide them into one of the frames inside the grooved edge. Secure the bottom rail to the side rails as you did the top rail, fitting the tin into the groove as you assemble the frame.

10. Fit the remaining frames with tin, and secure the bottom rails as described above.

11. Hinge the screen (see pages 15 and 16 for instructions).

John Garrett, *Stuff and Nonsense.* 1998. 80 x 84 x 6 in. (2 x 2.1 m x 15 cm). Screen made from various found, salvaged, and collected materials.

WELDED REBAR SCREEN

INSPIRED BY SOUTH AMERICAN TEXTILES PURCHASED ON A VACATION, THIS DESIGNER CAME UP WITH THIS SIMPLE BUT STRIKING WAY TO DISPLAY HER ACQUISITIONS BY HAVING A SCREEN FABRICATED FROM AN OLD DISCARDED PILE OF STEEL RODS. TO CREATE YOUR OWN DISPLAY SCREEN, USE THE PLANS PROVIDED, ALTERING THE WIDTH AND HEIGHT TO FIT YOUR TEXTILES OR FABRIC IF NEEDED.

Materials & Tools

3 long woven textiles or pieces of fabric that fit into the openings of your screen (the openings in the screen shown measure 15 x 61½ inches [38.1 cm x 1.5 m])

Screen plan (fig. 1)

Six ½-inch (1.3 cm) x 10-foot-long (3 m) pieces of steel rod (rebar) (available at home supply stores)

4 metal hinges, each measuring ¾ x 3 inches (1.9 x 7.6 cm) each

4 yards (3.6 m) of grosgrain ribbon to match your textiles or fabric

Thread to match textiles and ribbon

Sewing needle

Straight pins

Instructions

1 . Measure the height and width of your textiles or fabric that you plan to use as panels, and adjust the dimensions of the plan shown at the right to fit. Allow about 2 inches (5 cm) on each side for breathing room around the panels.

2 . Take the plan to several welding shops to get the best estimate for fabricating the screen with the rebar and the hinges.

3 . Once the screen is built to your specifications, cut the grosgrain ribbon into 8-inch (20.3 cm) strips. Position three strips on the back of each textile or fabric panel at the top and the bottom, spacing one in the center and the others 2 to 3 inches (5 to 7.6 cm) from the edge. The centers of the strips should be about 1 inch (2.5 cm) from the edges. Hold the ribbons in place with straight pins.

4 . Handsew two lines of stitching about ½ inch (1.3 cm) from the center of the width of each ribbon to secure them.

5 . Tie the panels to the screen using the ribbons.

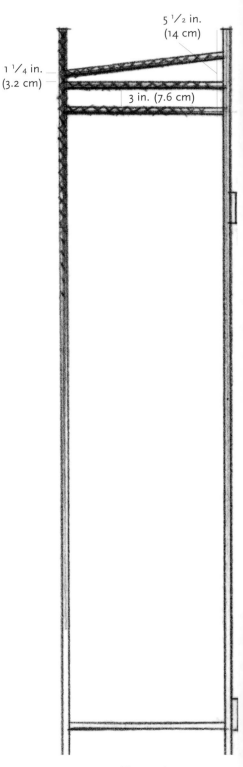

5 ½ in. (14 cm)

1 ¼ in. (3.2 cm)

3 in. (7.6 cm)

Figure 1

Gallery

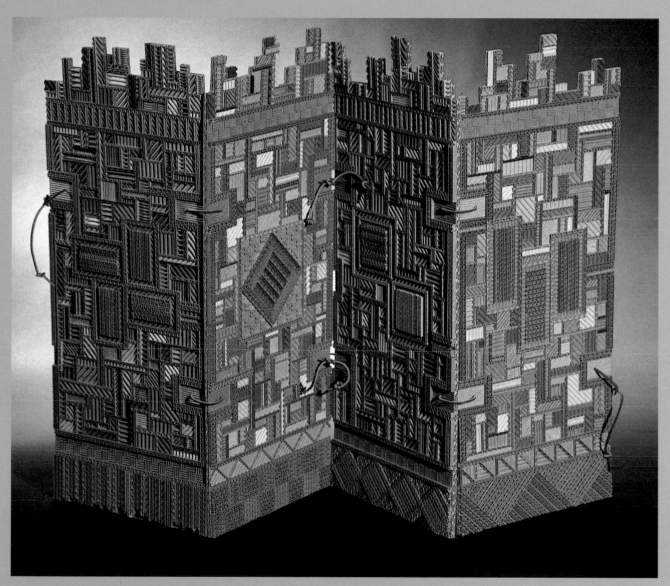

LUCI LYTLE, *Corrugated Mosaic Table Screen*. 2002. 30 x 48 x ½ IN. (76.2 x 00 x 1.3 CM). RECYCLED CORRUGATED CARDBOARD JOINED WITH RAWHIDE LACES COVERED WITH A CORRUGATED MOSAIC; ACRYLIC VARNISH. PHOTO BY KATE CAMERON.

DESIGNER: KARI LEE

RAWHIDE PHOTO TRANSFER SCREEN

WHETHER YOU WANT TO CAPTURE YOUR DREAM OF BEING A COWGIRL OR SIMPLY SHOW OFF FAMILY PHOTOS, YOUR VERSION OF THIS SCREEN WILL BE AN UNDISPUTED CONVERSATION PIECE. WHAT BEGAN AS A SET OF OLD WINDOWS IS MADE INTO AN UNUSUAL SCREEN FILLED WITH PANES MADE OF STRETCHED, PHOTO-TRANSFERRED RAWHIDE PIECES.

Materials & Tools

3 salvage windows or doors with panes of glass removed (windows shown measure 5½ feet high x 1½ feet wide [1.7 x .4 m])

Spray satin varnish

Measuring tape

Photos and fabric of your choice for image transfer

Straightedge/ruler

Pencil

Several pieces of poster board

Craft knife or knife made for cutting leather

Electric drill/screwdriver

³⁄₃₂ x ½-inch (2.4 mm x 1.3 cm) screw eyes

Screwdriver

Pliers

4 to 6 ounces (112 to 168 g) cream-colored rawhide

Large plastic tub

Several old towels

Punch board

¼-inch (6 mm) round drive punch and mallet

Grommet setter made for setting ⁵⁄₁₆-inch (8 mm) brass grommets (You must calculate the number needed for your particular piece after making the panel patterns described in step 2 of the directions.)

* (NOTE: YOU CAN FIND THE TOOLS AND LEATHERS LISTED ABOVE AT A LEATHER SUPPLY STORE OR ORDER THEM THROUGH A SUPPLIER. LOOK TO THE INTERNET AS A RESOURCE FOR A SUPPLIER, IF NEEDED.)

Instructions

1. Wash the surfaces of your doors or windows thoroughly to remove any dirt or flaking paint. Once dry, seal the surfaces with satin varnish.

2. Measure the inside dimensions of each window opening, and subtract 2 inches (5.1 cm) from the width and length. With the straightedge and a pencil, draw patterns on the poster board using the measurements. (If all the openings are the same, as they are on our piece, then you'll only need one pattern.) Cut out the patterns.

3. On the pattern(s), make marks around the edges that are spaced 2 inches (5.1 cm) apart and ½ inch (1.3 cm) from the edge. (These marks indicate where the grommets will go in the rawhide panels.)

4. Place the doors or windows flat on the floor, and position each of the patterns or the single pattern in the center of its opening. Inside the wooden frame, make pencil marks along the edges directly above or to the side of each of the pattern's grommet marks to indicate where the screw eyes will go. Use the handheld drill to predrill all of these holes inside the frame of

each window. Screw in each screw eye, and tighten it with pliers.

5. Fill the tub with clean water. Prepare the rawhide by soaking it until it becomes pliable. Transfer it to a large, clean cutting surface.

6. Use the poster board patterns, the straightedge, and a knife to cut out each rawhide panel. Dampen the towels, and place the panels between them to keep the waiting rawhide panels pliable as you work on each.

7. Place the punch board on your work surface. Use the ¼-inch (6 mm) round drive punch to punch holes in the rawhide where indicated on the pattern(s). Use the grommet setter and mallet to attach the grommets to each rawhide panel.

8. Next, you'll lace the sides of each rawhide panel to the screw eyes that you secured in each of the openings. Calculate how much lace to cut by multiplying the length of each inside edge (whether width or length) by three. Cut a corresponding piece of lace for each width or length.

9. Place the rawhide panels in each of their openings on the floor or your work surface. Thread one

end of the matching lace lengths by hand through the front of a corner grommet, and tie off the end of the lace on the back to hold it in place. Push the long end of the lace through the corresponding grommet from the back and out the front. Then move diagonally to the next hole up, and push the lace through the front of the grommet. Go back through the corresponding screw eye from the back. Continue this process until you reach the last hole on the other side of the panel. Make certain that the panel is still centered, and then tie off the other end of the lace so that it is taut but not tight. Check to make sure that it is about 2 inches (5.1 cm) from the center of each grommet hole to the center of each screw eye.

1 0 . Repeat this lacing process on the opposite side, pulling the lace taut but not tight. Lace the remaining two sides. Repeat this process to place the rawhide panels in all of the openings. After you've finished, allow the rawhide to dry completely.

1 1 . Photocopy the selected images onto pieces of transfer paper. Cut out the images. Arrange them on the panels as you would like them to be in the final piece.

1 2 . Soak each trimmed paper image in water for about a minute so that the film floats away from the paper. Use the foam roller to apply a light coat of turpentine to the surface of the rawhide where you plan to place the image.

1 3 . Carefully remove the film from the water, and place it between newsprint paper to remove the excess water. Slide each image off of the paper and gently position it on the rawhide.

Warning: The film will quickly adhere to the rawhide surface, so you won't be able to reposition it once it is placed.

1 4 . Use the paintbrush to apply a thin coat of turpentine to the image. Leave the screen flat until the rawhide is completely dry.

1 5 . Hinge the screen (see pages 15 and 16 for instructions.)

pages 15 and 16 for instructions.)

Materials & Tools

⅛-inch (3 mm) red latigo lace (You must calculate the amount needed as described in step 8 in the directions.)

Leather shears

Photocopies of desired images

Scissors

12 x 18-inch (30.5 x 45.7 cm) transfer paper made for artists (available at fine art supply stores)

Foam paint roller

2-inch (5.1 cm) paintbrush

Turpentine

Newsprint paper

6 double-acting/butterfly hinges with screws, each hinge measuring ¾ x 1¾ inches (1.9 x 4.4 cm)

CHINOISERIE SCREEN

B ITS OF ASIAN PAPERS AND IMAGES ARE PLAYFULLY COMBINED ON COMMON FOAM BOARD TO MAKE A TABLETOP SCREEN THAT LEAVES A LASTING IMPRESSION.

Materials & Tools

Metal ruler

Craft knife

Large piece of black foam board

Self-healing cutting mat

Asian images: images photocopied from copyright-free books, wrapping paper with Asian motifs, Chinese text (from a newspaper or photocopied from a book)

Scissors

Swatches of interesting papers such as colored tissue paper, textured handmade paper

PVA archival glue made for paper (available at art supply stores)

Small paintbrush for applying glue

Wax paper

Stack of books

Straight pins with colored glass heads (available at sewing or craft stores)

Small brass beads that fit on pins

1-inch-wide (2.5 cm) black masking tape

Instructions

1. Use the ruler and knife to measure and cut out three panels from the black foam board, each measuring 9 x 18½ inches (22.9 x 47 cm).

2. Place the panels vertically on your cutting mat. Measure and mark 1 x 7-inch (2.5 x 17.8 cm) openings an inch (2.5 cm) from the top and bottom of each panel. Use the craft knife and ruler to carefully cut them out. Remove the strips of board and save three of them.

3. Place the three panels side by side on your work surface. Choose images for each of your three panels. If needed, reduce or enlarge the images on a photocopy machine to fit your panels. (Make three copies of any that you plan to repeat on all three panels.) Trim the images as needed, and position them on the panels.

4. Cut out pieces of paper to fit the front of the three strips of board that you saved in step 2. Glue them to the front of each strip. Position the strips just underneath the top openings, and tear swatches of handmade paper to place behind them. Glue the

papers and strips of board into place.

5. Cut and tear bits of the tissue or handmade papers. Overlap these paper elements on your central motifs, creating a collage effect. Continue moving pieces of paper around until you are satisfied with the arrangement of the elements, keeping in mind the visual relationships between all of the panels as one composition.

6. After you've decided on the placement of the papers, use the brush to apply a thin coat of glue to the backs of each. Press the papers into place, carefully smoothing them out to remove any air bubbles. Brush glue on the remaining papers, and layer them on top. (Keep in mind that the glue will dry clear, so you need not worry about it streaking.)

7. Cover the panels with a sheet of wax paper followed by books to weigh down the glued papers as they dry. Allow to dry for several hours.

8. Slide a brass bead onto each of the pins with colored glass heads. Stick a series of them about 2 inches (5 cm) apart and straight down into the foam board along

the inside edges of the panel openings.

9. On a flat surface, space the panels about ¼ inch (6 mm) apart.

10. From the black masking tape, cut ½-inch-long (1.3 cm) tabs to hinge the panels together on the front in several places, spanning the ¼-inch (6 mm) openings between them. Turn the panels over flat and hinge them on the back as well. Adjust the panels as needed with the tape hinges, so that they are aligned.

11. Cut off three 20-inch (50.8 cm) lengths of black tape. Adhere them along the hinged seams on the front of the screen, allowing them to overlap the top and bottom edges. Cut three 18½-inch (47 cm) pieces of tape, and cover the seams on the back of the panel.

MICHALENE GROSHEK, *MARSH MAGIC*. 1988. 30 x 14 x 12 IN. (75 x 35 x 30 CM). HIGH-GRADE PLYWOOD SCREEN PRINTED AND STAINED WITH OIL-BASED PIGMENT; INNER FABRIC PANEL IS PIGMENT SCREENPRINTED AND HAND-PAINTED COTTON APPLIED TO WOOD; EMBELLISHED WITH COLOR PENCIL DRAWING; PAINTED BASSWOOD JOINING PIECES-METALLIC GOLD. PHOTO BY BILL LEMKE.

SPACE COLLAGE SCREEN

CREATE A THEMED SCREEN FOR A CHILD OR TEENAGER BY CLIPPING IMAGES FROM OLD MAGAZINES OR DISCARDED BOOKS. ALL YOU NEED IS SOME TIME, PAINT, AND GLUE TO MAKE A PIECE THAT ENGAGES THE SENSES AND IMAGINATION.

Materials & Tools

3 pieces of smooth ¾-inch (1.9 cm) ply-wood, each cut to 24 x 48 inches (61 cm x 1.2 m) (Begin with a 4 x 8-foot [1.2 x 2.4 m] piece of plywood and ask the salesperson at your home supply store or lumberyard to cut it in half lengthwise and widthwise to make the three panels—you'll have an extra panel left over.)

Space pictures from old magazines or salvage store books (such as stars, planets, nebulae, rockets)

Drop cloth

2 paint rollers

Paint tray with two disposable liners

Latex primer

Semigloss interior latex paint in black

2-inch-wide (5 cm) flat paintbrush

Artist's acrylic paint in white and orange

Clean rag

Scrap paper

Paper scissors

Decoupage medium

Rubber brayer (available in craft stores)

Pencil with eraser

4-inch-wide (10.2 cm) paintbrush

Clear acrylic gloss enamel

4 double-acting/butterfly hinges with screws, each hinge measuring ¾ x 1¾ inches (1.9 x 4.4 cm)

Electric drill/screwdriver

Instructions

1. Collect space images from magazines or old books.

2. Place a drop cloth on your work surface or the floor. Use a paint roller to apply latex primer to the three panels on both sides, allowing the first side to dry before painting the second.

3. Use a clean roller to paint the fronts, sides, and backs of each panel with the black latex paint, allowing the first side to dry thorougly before painting the second. Butt the panels together on the floor as they will appear once they are hinged.

4. Load the 2-inch-wide (5 cm) paintbrush with white acrylic paint that has been thinned slightly with water. Stand above the panels, and splatter a fine white spray of paint on each of the panels to create a starry background. Keep the paint light, and use a rag to wipe away any accidental drips. Allow it to dry. Wash out the brush.

5. Cut out pieces from your collected space images, and arrange them on the three panels, relating the elements to one another as if you're creating one large picture. Continue to move images around until you are satisfied with your composition.

6. To adhere the papers, remove them one at a time and place each on scrap paper before brushing a light coat of medium on the back with the 2-inch-wide (5 cm) paintbrush. Press the paper into position on the panel before firmly rolling it into place with the rubber brayer. Continue to roll back and forth to smooth out the paper and remove any air bubbles. Once you've applied all of the images, allow the glue to dry thoroughly.

7. To protect the images and ensure that they won't peel off later, paint a layer of medium over the pictures, and allow it to dry.

8. Dip the pencil eraser into the white acrylic paint, and add random white dots to the panels. Use orange acrylic paint to add a few orange dots and spirals. Allow the paint to dry.

9. Use the larger brush to apply a coat of the clear acrylic enamel to the front and sides of each panel. Allow the enamel to dry thoroughly before moving the panels.

10. Hinge the screen (see pages 15 and 16 for instructions).

LISA HOUCK, *A TORNADO WATCH IS IN EFFECT.* 1991. 62 x 48 IN. (1.6 x 1.2 M). OIL PAINT ON WOOD PANELS.

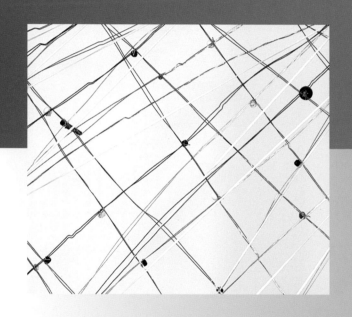 

AIRY AND REVEALING

A SCREEN CAN BE REVEALING AS WELL AS CONCEALING. THIS SECTION WILL GIVE YOU LOTS OF IDEAS, INCLUDING HOW TO MAKE A COLORFUL SUSPENDED BANNER THAT DOUBLES AS A DIVIDER, STRING WIRE AND BEADS ON OPEN FRAMES TO MAKE A SOPHISTICATED CONVERSATION PIECE, OR TRANSFORM OLD PLASTIC NOTEBOOK SLEEVES INTO A HANGING TREASURE TROVE FOR PERSONAL KEEPSAKES. YOU'LL THINK ABOUT SCREENS IN A NEW WAY AFTER YOU THUMB THROUGH THIS SECTION.

WOVEN WIRE AND BEAD SCREEN

T HIS GORGEOUS SCREEN WOVEN FROM COLORED WIRES, RIBBON, AND GLASS BEADS SHIMMERS WITH REFLECTED LIGHT. ALTHOUGH TIME-CONSUMING, IT ISN'T DIFFICULT TO MAKE.

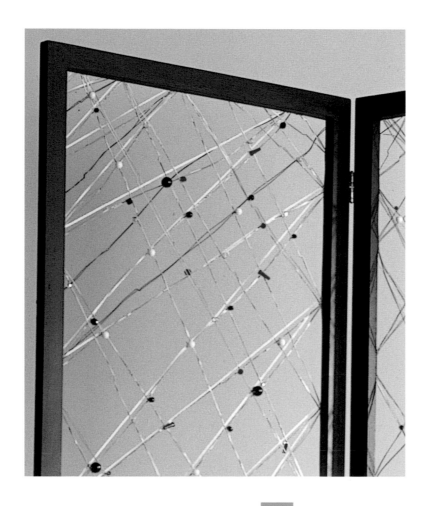

Materials & Tools

2 frames made of 1¼ x ¾-inch (3.2 x 1.9 cm) wood pieces; each measures 20½ x 64 inches (52 x 162.6 cm) after assembly (see pages 13 to 15 for instructions and tools)

1-inch-wide (2.5 cm) flat paintbrush

Black satin latex paint

Piece of white chalk

Clamps (optional)

9 rolls of 20-gauge copper wire, 135 yards (121 m) total

Staple gun with ¼-inch (6 mm) staples

Wire cutters

45 yards (40.5 m) of white ⅛-inch-wide (3 mm) ribbon

Scissors

2 rolls of 20-gauge red wire, 30 yards (27 m) total

Hot glue gun and glue sticks

4 strips of 1-inch-wide (2.5 cm) plain black ribbon, each 64 inches (162.6 cm) long

4 strips of 1-inch-wide (2.5 cm) plain black ribbon, each 20 inches (50.8 cm) long

6 double-acting/butterfly hinges with screws, each hinge measuring ¾ x 1¾ inches (1.9 x 4.4 cm)

Electric drill/screwdriver

Assorted glass beads in white, red, and black that fit on 24-gauge wire

24-gauge steel wire cut into 2-inch-long (5 cm) strips, one for each glass bead that you attach

Instructions

1. Use the 1-inch-wide (2.5 cm) paintbrush to apply one or two coats of the black satin paint to the frames. Allow the frames to dry thoroughly.

2. Place one of the frames flat on your work surface. Beginning at one end of both the top and bottom of the frame, use the chalk to mark six points in the center of the wood, spacing them apart about 2½ to 3 inches (6.4 to 7.6 cm) each. Vary the width of each slightly.

3. Along the sides of the frame, use the chalk to mark 10 points in the center that are spaced apart about 4 to 6 inches (10.2 to 15.2 cm) each, varying the spacing slightly as you did on the widths. Mark the remaining two panels with the same marks.

4. Place one of the frames on your work surface with the chalk marks facing you. (You may wish to clamp the edges of the frame to your work surface.)

5. Unroll a portion of the copper wire. Staple one end of it to the first mark on the left side of the top of the frame, leaving a ½-inch (1.3 cm) wire tail. Fold the tail down over the staple, and staple it again to lock the wire in place.

6. Stretch the wire in a diagonal to the first mark at the top of the left vertical side of the frame. Using the marks as reference points, continue stapling the wire back and forth across the screen until you reach the bottom of the panel. Bend the wire randomly as you're stretching it to create lightning-bolt-shaped crimps in the wire. When you're finished, lock the end of the wire in place as you did at the top of the panel before cutting it with wire cutters. Repeat this process to double the copper wire across the screen.

7. Beginning on the opposite side of the frame (right side), staple the end of the copper wire to the first mark on the top, overlapping the copper wires already in place. Lock the wire in place. Repeat step 6 to string another set of diagonally placed copper wires onto the frame from the opposite direction.

8. Unroll a length of the 1/8-inch-wide (3 mm) white ribbon. Follow the path of the copper wire that you strung in step 6, using the same stapling techniques to attach the ribbon. Cut the ribbon with scissors when you reach the bottom.

9. Unroll a length of the red wire to use as an accent to the wires and ribbon you've already placed. Randomly attach a few lines of red wire in both directions between the diagonals that you've created at the top and the bottom of the frame, crimping the wires as you wish. Repeat to double the red wire.

10. Repeat steps 4 through 9 for the second panel in the frame, reversing the side on which you begin attaching the copper wire.

11. Flip each frame over, and hot glue the lengths of black ribbon over the staples on the frame.

12. Hinge the screen (see pages 15 and 16 for instructions).

13. Stand the screen up so that you can attach the glass beads to the front. String beads onto the 2-inch-long (5 cm) pieces of 24-gauge steel wire. Bend the wires in the middle so that the bead sits in the center of each. Twist the ends of the wire tightly around intersecting points of the strung wires on both frames so that the beads hang on the front.

A VIEW OF THE SCREEN FROM THE BACK.

DESIGNER: KATHERINE AIMONE

EASY FABRIC
SCREEN

A DECEPTIVELY SIMPLE YET EFFECTIVE LIGHTWEIGHT FABRIC SCREEN PROVIDES AN ATTRACTIVE WAY TO CAMOUFLAGE THE OPENING BETWEEN TWO SPACES. THE STRIPS OF LONG FABRIC CAN BE MOVED TO PRO-VIDE DIFFERENT COVERAGE AND LOOKS. (THE CURTAIN ROD'S WIDE SPAN PROVIDES ROOM TO MOVE THE FABRIC AWAY FROM THE DOOR WHEN NOT NEEDED.)

Instructions

1. Mount your curtain rod at the height that you want.

2. Measure the length from the floor to the bottom of the rod and add about 6 inches (15.2 cm) to this number. Use this measurement to cut the length of three or more pieces of fabric, varying the widths of the fabrics slightly.

3. Fold over and iron a narrow hem toward the underside on all four sides of each panel. Turn the seam over again on all sides except the bottom to hide the cut edges. Use straight lines of stitching to sew the seam close to the fold on the tops of all panels. Overlap the side seams at the corners, and sew those seams into place in the same manner.

4. On the bottom of each panel, iron up a wide hem of about 8 inches (20.3 cm) to provide weight on the bottom of each panel and clear the floor. Pin the hem in place, and hand or machine stitch it in place.

5. Attach the curtain rings with clips to the tops of the panels at evenly spaced intervals of about 3 inches (7.6 cm).

6. Slide the curtain panels onto the rod, and place the panels as desired. If you wish, you can overlap the edges of the panels by alternating the clips on two adjacent panel edges.

Materials & Tools

Wall-mounted curtain rod or spring rod (long enough to span the space that you want to cover, as well as provide room to move fabric pieces back and forth)

Measuring tape

Fabric scissors

Long lengths of lightweight, semi-sheer fabrics of your choice (we used three patterned fabrics)

Clothes iron

Sewing machine and thread that matches fabrics

Straight pins

Curtain rod clips or curtain rings (as many as you need to attach the widths of the fabric pieces)

DESIGNER: DIANA LIGHT

WOVEN RIBBON SCREEN

WEAVE RIBBONS ONTO FRAMES TO CREATE INTERESTING PAT-TERNS THAT SOFTLY VEIL A SECTION OF A ROOM.

Materials & Tools

3 frames made of 1¼ x ¾-inch (3.2 x 1.9 cm) wood pieces; each measures 20½ x 64 inches (52 x 162.6 cm) after assembly (see pages 13 to 15 for instructions and tools)

Drop cloth

1½-inch-wide (3.8 cm) flat paintbrush

Acrylic latex enamel primer

Acrylic latex high-gloss enamel in almond

10 assorted rolls of ribbon in various widths and colors, at least 10 yards (9 m) each

Staple gun and staples

Scissors

Hot glue gun and glue sticks

14 yards (12.6 m) of flat, braided cording in color that complements the ribbons

4 double-acting/butterfly hinges with screws, each hinge measuring ¾ x 1¾ inches (1.9 x 4.4 cm)

Electric screwdriver/drill

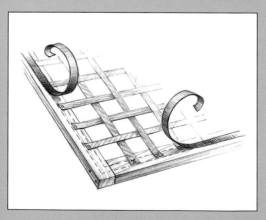

Figure 1

Instructions

1. Place the drop cloth on your work surface or on the floor. Use the paintbrush to apply a coat of primer to all sides of the frames. Allow it to dry completely.

2. Paint the frame with the almond-colored paint, and allow it to dry.

3. Lay one of the painted panels flat on your work surface.

4. Choose one of the ribbons, and staple one end of it a short distance inside the opening of the frame in the middle of the wood on the shorter side (see figure 1 below).

5. Roll the ribbon across the frame's opening to the other side, keeping the ribbon parallel to the length of the frame. Stretch it tight, and staple it to the other side in the middle of the wood. Cut off the end of it close to the staple. Continue to add strips of each kind of ribbon in this way, spacing them apart as you wish until the width of the frame is filled with vertical ribbons. Repeat this process with the ribbons on the remaining two frames, keeping them in the same order or varying the order of them.

6. On one of the long sides, staple the end of one of the rolls of ribbon as you did in step 4. Weave the ribbon through the long strips, moving in and out until you reach the other side of the frame. Pull it tight, make sure that it is parallel to the short side of the frame, then staple it to the middle of the wood on the other side of the frame. Cut off the excess ribbon.

7. Continue to weave, stretch, and staple a pattern of ribbons across the length of your frame, spacing them apart as you wish.

8. Repeat steps 4 through 7 to fill the other two panels with woven ribbon, either repeating or varying the pattern that you created in the first panel.

9. Use hot glue to attach a line of flat braided cord around the face of each frame to cover the staples, cutting it at the corners and overlapping it (see figure 1). Allow the glue to dry.

10. Hinge the screen (see pages 15 and 16 for instructions).

Gallery

FAYE ZHANG, *BLUE BIRD.*
(FRONT: BELOW. BACK:
ABOVE.) 2001. 8 x 10
FT. (2.4 x 3 M).
HANDWOVEN TAPESTRY
WITH METALLIC THREADS,
SILK, AND RAYON.
PHOTO BY ARTIST.

DESIGNER: LUANN UDELL

RICE PAPER
SHADE SCREEN

DECORATE A PAPER SHADE WITH ROUGHLY TORN AND COLLAGED SHAPES, AND YOU'LL CREATE AN ARTISTIC SCREEN THAT ALLOWS LIGHT TO SHINE THROUGH WHEN IT'S SUSPENDED.

Materials & Tools

Rice paper shade in desired size (Note: Many paper shades are now made of a synthetic fiber rather than real rice fiber, which doesn't make a good surface for gluing. Look for a shade that is made of real paper so that the collage pieces will adhere easily.)

Soft pencil

Scrap paper

Large black marker

Several sheets of solid-colored, hand-made papers

Small paintbrush

Jar of water

Old sheet (optional)

1-inch-wide (2.5 cm) flat paintbrush

Permanent PVA archival glue

Clean, damp rag

Small rubber brayer (optional)

Clear fishing line or thin wire

Ceiling hooks or spring rod made for bath or curtains

Instructions

1. Sketch out some simple, broad shapes for the design on your shade. (The motifs in this project were enlarged from a set of rubber stamp images, so look around for a design that you like, or make up your own.) Draw each design in pencil on a separate sheet of scrap paper, then outline it with the large black marker.

2. To transfer each shape onto the colored paper, place it underneath the paper of your choice. (You should be able to see the bold outline of the shape underneath the paper.) Dip the small paintbrush in water, and follow the lines of the image as you trace it onto the handmade paper.

3. Gently pull the handmade papers apart along the wet lines. (The paper should gently tear in a soft, deckled edge.) If the water dries before you finish tearing, simply retrace the image with the paintbrush. Paint and tear as many designs in various colors as you want for your hanging screen.

4. Unroll the rice paper shade onto a large, flat work surface or onto a sheet spread out on the floor. If you don't want to use the roll-up hardware that comes on the shade, remove it, but leave the hanging hooks at the top of the shade.

5. Position the torn-paper shapes in a pleasing pattern across the shade. If you're using a table, you may want to stand on a stepstool or chair for a better view of the whole shade while you decide where to place the shapes.

6. Once you've placed the shapes, remove them one at a time from the shade to apply glue to them. To do this, place each shape on a sheet of scrap paper, and use the 1-inch (2.5 cm) flat paintbrush to gently brush a thin coat of glue onto the reverse side. Quickly place the shape, glue side down, in position on the screen. Keep the damp rag handy for wiping excess glue from your fingers so that they don't stick to the papers as you glue them. When you're finished gluing, rinse and clean the flat paintbrush, leaving it slightly damp.

7. Use the tips of your fingers to gently press and smooth each motif in place on the shade. Use the damp paintbrush to feather out the edges of each motif. (When partially dry, follow up by smoothing the shapes with a small brayer, if you wish.)

8. Allow the screen to dry completely. To hang it, use the clear fishing line or thin wire to attach it to hooks in the ceiling or a spring rod in a doorway or other opening.

Gallery

JOHN M. DEHOOG, *INTERACTIVE SHOJI* (TWO VIEWS). 1997. 82 x 64 x 1 IN. (205 x 160 x 2.5 CM).
SCREEN MADE OF 24 MOVEABLE PANELS OF WHITE PINE AND JAPANESE HANDMADE PAPER; MORTISE-AND-TENON JOINERY.
PHOTO BY ARTIST.

OPULENT SILK SCREEN

BOLD PAINTED DESIGNS MAKE A VISUAL STATEMENT ON THIS THREE-PANELED SILK SCREEN THAT CAPITALIZES ON THE EFFECTS OF WARM METALLICS ON A COOL BACKGROUND.

Materials & Tools

Metal screen with open panels (available through home decor stores, furniture stores, and home supply stores)

Measuring tape

Raw silk in two colors of your choice, one color for main sections of the panels and the other for contrasting borders (see instructions to determine the amount of fabric to buy)

White fabric marker or chalk

Straightedge

Fabric scissors

Old bed covering, mattress pad, carpet padding, or other surface on which to paint on

Roll of freezer paper

Clothes iron

Designs of your choice (we based ours on designs found in copyright-free design books)

¼ and ½-inch-wide (6 mm and 1.3 cm) flat, synthetic artist's brushes

Metallic fabric paints (we used antique gold and gold)

Foam roller with decorative border design (available at home supply and paint stores) or repeating pattern/border foam stamp of your choice

Sewing machine with thread that matches border silk

Small safety pins

Instructions

1. Use a measuring tape to determine the height of the space inside one of the openings on your screen. Measure the width as well, and subtract about 2 inches (5 cm) from each side to leave some breathing room for your panel once it is hung. Use these measurements to figure out how much silk yardage you need to buy for the panels. (Our finished panels measure 17 x 52 inches [43.2 cm x 1.3 m].)

2. Purchase contrasting border silk that is at least the length of one of your panels. This will provide you with enough silk to sew the borders. Do not prewash your silk before painting it.

3. Use a fabric marker or piece of chalk and a straightedge to mark off the boundaries of the panels on the larger piece of silk. Cut out the panels.

4. Cover the surface of a large table or other surface with an old clean sheet or other fabric. Roll out a sections of freezer paper to cover the backs of your panels.

5. Set your iron on a low setting, and lightly iron freezer paper onto the back of each panel from the fabric side. (The paper will make your silk stiff so that it is easier to paint.)

6. On the front of the silk, use the fabric marker or chalk and the straightedge to draw lines on each panel indicating the width of the top and bottom borders (ours are 5 inches [12.7 cm] wide). You should make a border wide enough to contain the border stamp that you plan to use. Leave these marked off areas blank when you paint the main panels.

7. Beginning with the larger artist's brush, paint the main lines of your design on the silk panels using the metallic paints. Use the smaller brush to paint the detailed areas. Allow the paint to dry thoroughly on all of the panels. Remove the paper from the backs of the panels.

8. For each panel, cut two pieces of silk from the border fabric that measure the width of the border you marked in step 6, plus 1 inch (2.5 cm), and the width of the panel, plus 1 inch (2.5 cm).

9. Iron freezer paper onto the back of the border pieces.

10. Use the foam roller with the border design or the border stamp

to roll or stamp a pattern in paint across the border pieces. Allow the paint to dry, and remove the paper from the back.

1 1 . Iron under the long edges of all of the border pieces with a ½-inch (1.3 cm) seam. Set them aside.

1 2 . To make the tabs for tying the panels in place, cut strips of border fabric that measure 1 x 18 inches (2.5 x 45.7 cm) each. Cut eight strips for each panel.

1 3 . Fold the strips in half width-wise, and machine sew a ¼-inch-wide (6 mm) seam along the length of each. Turn the strips inside-out by attaching a small safety pin to the end of each and pushing it through the tube out the other side.

1 4 . After turning all of the tabs, iron them so that the seam is along one edge. Topstitch close to the edge to finish them, and fold them in half lengthwise so that they are doubled over on themselves.

1 5 . Along the tops of the front of each panel, pin the fold of each tab into position ½ inch (1.3 cm) in from the edge, spacing four tabs apart evenly on each end. Repeat this process for the bottom of each panel.

1 6 . Place the painted border pieces faceup on top of the areas that you marked off for them. (You'll cover the fold in the tabs when you do this.) Topstitch the border pieces in place close to the edge on both the top and the bottom, securing the tabs.

1 7 . For each panel, cut two long pieces of border fabric the length of your panels plus ¼ inch (6 mm) and around 2½ inches (6.4 cm) wide. Iron under all edges

¼ inch (6 mm) before pressing the border pieces in half lengthwise. Position the borders along each side of the panel, overlapping the edges of the panels. Topstitch the borders into place along the inside edges (see figure 1 below).

1 8 . Tie the panels to the metal bars at the top and bottom of each panel, pulling the panels taut.

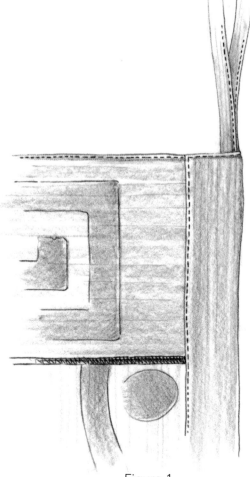

Figure 1

SHEER FABRIC SCREEN

Translucent fabrics are over-lapped on a background of sheer voile using an easy technique. The screen provides minimal cover-age, veiling the objects behind it. (The curved edges and joinery of this screen can be cut and assem-bled by an experienced carpenter, or you can assemble an easy-to-make rectangular screen instead.)

Materials & Tools

3-panel wooden frame screen with curved edge (see figure 1 below for the curve to cut for middle and side panels) or substitute a simple-to-make 3-panel rectangular screen (see pages 13 to 15 for the instructions and tools)

Several old bed sheets

Light pink voile or any sheer non-stretch fabric in yardage that will fill the open spaces of the frames (Along the outside edge of the wood frames of each panel, measure the height at the HIGHEST point of each and combine it with the width of each to determine the size of each panel to cut—then figure your overall yardage based on the combination of these sizes.)

Fabric marking pen or chalk

Fabric scissors

Staple gun and staples

Scissors

Flower template enlarged to size that fits your screen panels (see figure 2 on page 115)

Fusible webbing, 2 yards (1.8 m)

3 solid-colored fabrics of similar weight as panel fabric in light pink, medium pink, and a darker hot pink, 1 yard (.9 m) of each

Clothes iron

1-inch-wide (2.5 cm) pink ribbon or bias tape (determine yardage by measuring all the way around each frame and adding up the measurements)

Hot glue gun and glue sticks

4 double-acting/butterfly hinges with screws that fit the size of your screen

Electric drill/screwdriver

Instructions

1. On a large work surface (such as a table or a large piece of smooth plywood covered with an old sheet), spread out one end of the pink sheer fabric. Place one of the open frames facedown on top of it, leaving plenty of fabric to cut out the other two panels.

2. Trace around the outside of the frame with the marking pen or chalk, adding a 1-inch (2.5 cm) margin. Trace the remaining two panels in the same way, making sure to leave a margin all the way around.

3. Carefully cut out each panel.

4. Place one of the frames facedown on your work surface, draped with the panel that fits it. Once the fabric is placed so that it completely covers the frame and leaves a margin hanging over the edge, you're ready to staple it to the back of the frame.

5. Staple the fabric at the centerpoints of all four sides, pulling the fabric taut as you proceed. (Position the head of your staple gun in the center of the wood at a diagonal when stapling so that the staples will hold the fabric more securely.) Continue to gently pull and staple the fabric from these points around the edges of the frame, spacing the staples about ½ inch (1.3 cm) apart.

6. In the same fashion, staple the other sheer panels to the backs of the two remaining frames.

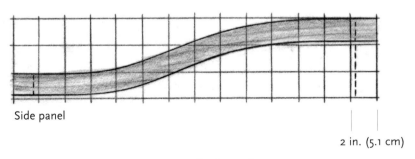

Side panel

Figure 1

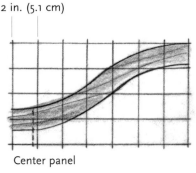

2 in. (5.1 cm)

2 in. (5.1 cm)

Center panel

7. Trim away the excess fabric close to the staples all the way around each frame.

8. Lay out an old sheet on the floor, and place the panels side by side and faceup on the floor.

9. Cut out the overlapping flower templates, and use the fabric marking pen or chalk to trace one set of them onto the fusible webbing. Cut a wide margin around each of the shapes without cutting out the details.

10. Assemble the three solid-colored fabrics on your work surface. Iron each of the templates onto a different color of fabric. Cut out the shapes that you drew on the back of the webbing.

11. Repeat steps 9 and 10 to create several more flowers, varying the colors of the parts as seen in the finished photo of the screen.

12. Position the flowers faceup on the screen while it is on the floor. In a couple of places, allow the flowers to overlap the frame, and use your scissors to cut away the portions that overlap so that the remaining portions of the flowers seem to disappear behind the frame (see the finished photo). Use

this same technique to create the illusion of cropped flowers around the edges.

13. Once the flowers are positioned, cut out curved stem shapes with buds from the solid-colored fabrics to connect the flowers and create movement in the design.

14. Cover your worktable with a sheet, and lift one of the frames up, keeping it in a horizontal position with the flowers and stems in place. Slide it onto the table. Set your iron to a setting that is appropriate for the fusible webbing (read the manufacturer's instructions). Gently iron

the flowers and stems onto the sheer panel fabric. Slide the panel around as needed to reach all the pieces.

15. After you've ironed the pieces of your design into place, flip each frame over on your table and cut out strips of ribbon or bias tape to cover the staples. Use the hot glue gun to draw beads of glue along the edges of the frame. Press the strips of ribbon or bias tape into place.

16. Hinge the screen (see pages 15 and 16 for instructions).

1¹⁄₄ in.
(5.1 cm)

Figure 2

WIRE WEB SCREEN

A WEB OF SILVER WIRE STRUNG RANDOMLY WITHIN THREE FRAMES CREATES A SUBTLE, REVEALING SCREEN THAT IS A BEAUTIFUL SCULPTURAL OBJECT.

Materials & Tools

Sawhorses and large piece of plywood or other large work surface

6 boards, each 1 x 2 inches (2.5 x 5 cm) x 63½ inches (1.6 m) to serve as legs

Measuring tape

Medium C-clamps

6 boards, each 1 x 2 inches (2.5 x 5.1 cm) x 18 inches (45.7 cm) to serve as crosspieces

Small carpenter's square

Electric drill/screwdriver

1-inch (2.5 cm) wood screws

Wood putty

Small putty knife

Sandpaper

Small electric sander (optional)

Black spray enamel

4 double-acting/butterfly hinges with screws, each hinge measuring ¾ x 1¾ inches (1.9 x 4.4 cm)

Black acrylic paint

Paintbrush

6 yards (5.5 m) of 28-gauge wire in silver

Wire cutters

Needle-nose pliers

#4 thumbtacks

Instant epoxy

Small C-clamps

Silver-colored craft wire

Instructions

1 . On your work surface, place the legs side-by-side with the shorter sides facing up. Stretch the measuring tape from the top of each leg down the length, and make marks at 1⅛ inches (2.8 cm) and 19⅛ inches (48.6 cm). Separate the legs into pairs.

2 . Clamp one of the legs to your work surface with its shorter side up, aligning it with the straight edge of your plywood surface or other surface. Place two of the crosspieces at right angles next to the marks that you made on the leg. Check the angles with the carpenter's square to make sure that the boards are perpendicular to one another. To create the frame, position another leg on the other side of the boards already in place, aligning the marks on that side as well. Check the angles again.

3 . Along the outside face of each leg, make two marks across the width (about ½ inch [1.3 cm] from each edge) to indicate where each crosspiece connects.

4 . Follow the guidelines outlined on pages 13 to 15 to drill pilot holes and screw the assembly together.

5 . When all of the frames have been assembled, cover the screws with wood putty to disguise them, and allow the putty to dry. Sand the entire frames, including where you've applied wood putty.

6 . In a well-ventilated area or outside, spray the frames with an even coat of black spray enamel. Spray the hinges with a coat of enamel as well. Allow the enamel to dry thoroughly.

7 . Following the guidelines on pages 15 and 16, hinge the frames together to make your screen. Camouflage the ends of the screws by brushing a bit of black acrylic paint on each.

8 . Now that your frame is assembled, sketch three boxes to represent your frame. Draw loose boxes within the squares to represent your wire anchor bars. Like the random nature of a spider web, these shapes needn't be predictable or repetitive. Be creative!

9 . Use the wire cutters to cut the silver wire into lengths of about 2 yards (1.8 m) each, one for each frame. With the help of needle-nose pliers, wrap the end of each piece around a thumbtack. Loosely following your sketch, attach the

wire end to the first anchor point on a frame, pushing the tack into the middle of the inside ledge. (Push the tack in just enough to hold at this point.) Stretch the wire loosely to the next point, wrap a thumbtack, and push the next into place. Continue this process until you've made your way around the frame. Clip the wire ends at the first and last tack.

10. One by one, pull each thumbtack out momentarily while you squeeze a bit of epoxy into the holes. Push each tack back into place. Use small C-clamps to hold the tacks firmly in place until the epoxy has set.

11. Now that the anchor wires are in place, begin to build a web at any point on one of the frames by attaching the end of the silver craft wire with several wraps. Work randomly with the silver wire, looping the wire over onto itself and stretching it in different directions as you weave in and out of the anchor bars. Use the same technique to spin a web on the remaining two frames.

12. Drizzle drops of epoxy to hold the wires more firmly in place and to simulate dew on the web.

Gallery

JILL HENRIETTA DAVIS, *ROOM DIVIDER*. 1998. 72 x 48 x 6 IN. (180 x 120 x 15 CM). BLOWN, CUT, POLISHED, AND ASSEMBLED GLASS; SCREEN SUSPENDED BY WIRES. PHOTO BY ARTIST.

QUILT DESIGN HANGING SCREEN

COMPOSE AN EYE-CATCHING ABSTRACT DESIGN FROM FABRIC SWATCHES TO MAKE A BANNER THAT CAN BE HUNG AS A SCREEN THAT PROVIDES A VISUAL "BREAK" IN A ROOM. THIS PROJECT USES FUSIBLE WEBBING TO ATTACH AND EMBELLISH THE FABRIC TO ITS BACKING WITHOUT A LOT OF FUSS.

Materials & Tools

Measuring tape

Heavyweight muslin, cotton, or linen for front of screen and backing fabric in color of your choice for back of screen (see steps 1 and 2 in the instructions to determine yardage)

Fabric scissors

Clothes iron

Sewing machine with thread

Straight pins

Fabric swatches in assorted colors and patterns (we used custom-dyed and silkscreened fabrics and ribbons, but any solid or patterned fabrics will do)

Fusible webbing

Lengths of decorative ribbon in several colors to complement your fabrics

Freehand embroidery foot for sewing machine

Embroidery threads in several colors to complement your fabrics

1-inch (2.5 cm) wooden or copper dowel in length that is 2 inches (5 cm) longer than the width of your screen (see step 1 of the intructions)

Clear fishing line or thin wire

Pocket knife or other small knife

Ceiling hooks (made for hanging plants)

INSTRUCTIONS

1 . After you decide on the placement of your hanging screen, determine the length and width that you want it to be, taking into account your ceiling height and the space that you want to leave underneath it.

2 . From the muslin or cotton, cut a piece that is 2 inches (5 cm) wider and longer than the size you calculated. From the backing fabric, cut a piece that is 2 inches (5 cm) wider and 4 inches (10.2 cm) longer, to allow for the addition of a sleeve at the top.

3 . On one of the ends of the backing fabric, turn the cloth under ½-inch (1.3 cm), and iron it into place. Close to the edge, sew a zigzag stitch 1½ inches (3.8 cm) down each side to prevent fraying later. Fold over another hem that is 2 inches (5 cm) wide. Use your machine to sew a straight seam close to the edge of the hem to create a pocket for the dowel.

4 . Place the other piece of cloth on your work surface. From your fabrics, cut swatches in various shapes and sizes, and arrange them like a collage on your cloth "canvas" to create the main visual focus points of your composition. (You can add smaller, more detailed pieces later.) Pin them in place so that you can hold the banner up and study their placement.

5 . Once you are satisfied with the position of the main pieces, cut out fusible webbing to back each of them. Sandwich the webbing between the fabrics, and then iron the pieces into place on the front, following the manufacturer's instructions.

6 . Cut out more pieces of fabric, and add another layer to your composition, overlapping them as you wish. When you're finished, fuse them to the other fabrics.

7 . Cut pieces of ribbon, and twist and turn them on top of the fabric shapes. Tack them loosely into place with straight pins.

8 . Attach the freehand embroidery foot to your machine, and slowly sew on the ribbons, removing the pins as you go. Don't worry about sewing them perfectly; allow them to twist and move. By hand, stitch decorative threads to the banner, creating designs that crisscross the various fabric pieces. Leave threads hanging as you wish. Continue to add fabrics, ribbons,

and threads until you're satisfied with your fabric collage.

9. Turn under a ½-inch (1.3 cm) hem at the top of the front piece, and iron it into place. Place the front and back panels together with the right sides facing one another. Sew the two sides and bottoms together with a ½-inch (1.3 cm) seam.

10. Turn the banner inside out through the opening in the top. Insert the dowel into the pocket, then slip stitch the front to the back at the top.

11. Cut a notch in each dowel with the pocket knife to hold the fishing line or wire in place. Tie a length of fishing line or thin wire to each end of the dowel within the grooves, and suspend the screen from the ceiling on ceiling hooks.

Gallery

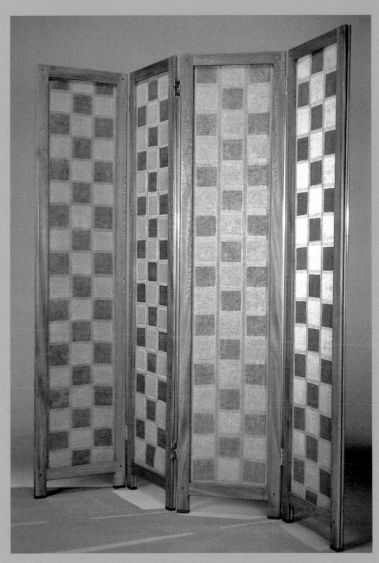

SUZANNE AND JOHN GERNANDT, *PAPER LIGHT SCREEN.* 6 x 6½ FT. (1.8 x 2 M) x 1 IN. (2.5 CM). DOUBLE-SIDED FRAME CONSTRUCTED OF SYCAMORE AND MAHOGANY; PANELS OF HAND-DYED LINEN WOVEN IN 12-HARNESS DOUBLE-WEAVE STRUCTURE, HANDMADE PAPER INSERTED INTO DOUBLE-WOVEN "POCKETS"; JAPANESE SHOJI HINGES. PHOTO BY TIM BARNWELL.

PAINTED DESKTOP SCREENS

T HE DESIGNER OF THESE SCREENS LOVES TO PAINT ON SMALL, PORTABLE PIECES OF PLYWOOD. HINGED TOGETHER INTO ACCOR-DION-LIKE PIECES THAT MIMIC LARGER SCREENS, THEY PROVIDE A VISUAL ACCENT FOR ANY DESK, SHELF, TABLE, OR MANTLE.

INSTRUCTIONS

1. Sand the surfaces and edges of the plywood with the medium-grit sandpaper. When finished, wipe the boards with a damp sponge or rag to remove the dust.

2. Mark the placement of the hinges at ⅜ inch (9.5 mm) from the top and bottom edges of each three-part screen. Use a 1/16-inch (1.6 mm) bit to drill small pilot holes through the marks on the boards for the screws. Fasten the hinges to the boards, using the guidelines on pages 15 and 16.

3. Use the flat paintbrush to apply gesso or wood primer to the entire screen, including the hinges.

4. When the gesso has dried, use the paintbrushes and acrylic paints to paint a design of your choice on one side of each screen. Paint designs that relate to one another, since the two screens will be shown as a pair. Add a bit of acrylic medium to the paints as you go along to keep them wet while you work and make them more fluid. Experiment with layering the paint and applying it with alternating wet and dry brushes. Scratch the surface with the end of one of your paintbrushes to reveal the layers.

5. After the paint dries, scribble lines and marks over the surface with the black marker.

6. After one side of the screens has dried, paint the reverse sides.

7. Apply a coat of acrylic gloss medium to all of the surfaces of the screens as a final step.

MATERIALS & TOOLS

6 pieces of ⅜-inch (9.5 mm) smooth plywood, each cut to 5 x 5 inches (12.7 cm x 12.7 cm x 9.5 mm) or size of your choice

Medium-grit sandpaper

Sponge or rag

4 double-acting/butterfly hinges with screws, each hinge measuring 11/16 x ¾ inches (1.7 x 1.9 cm)

Drill with 1/16-inch (1.6 mm) bit

1-inch-wide (2.5 cm) flat paintbrush

Gesso (available at art supply stores) or white wood primer

Small and medium-sized artists' paintbrushes

Acrylic paints in colors of your choice (red, yellow, blue, and white can be mixed to make any colors that you want)

Fine-tip permanent black marker

Acrylic gloss medium

WAX PAPER SCREEN

REMEMBER PRESSING CRAYON SHAVINGS BETWEEN WAX PAPER TO SIMULATE STAINED GLASS WHEN YOU WERE A CHILD? IF NOT, MAYBE YOU PRESSED AUTUMN LEAVES BETWEEN WAX PAPER TO PRESERVE THEM. THE BEAUTIFUL, LUMINOUS PAPER THAT DECORATES THIS SCREEN USES THE SAME TECHNIQUE.

Materials and Tools

3-part unassembled manufactured
wooden screen with dowels for holding
fabric or paper*

Sandpaper

Old newspapers

Medium-sized flat paintbrush

Acrylic wood primer

Latex house paint in color of your choice

Clear polyurethane wood sealer

4 double-acting/butterfly hinges with
screws (each hinge measuring $^{11}/_{16}$ x
$^3/_4$ inches (1.7 x 1.9 cm)

Electric drill/screwdriver

Old beach towel

Wax paper

Scissors

Tissue papers in various colors of your
choice

Clothes iron

Hot glue gun and glue sticks

*THE TRADITIONAL CHANGING SCREEN THAT WE
USED CAN BE ORDERED FROM WALNUT HOLLOW
WOODCRAFTS, 1409 STATE ROAD 23,
DODGEVILLE, WISCONSIN, 53533-2112;
PHONE: (608) 935-2341, FAX: (608) 935-3029

INSTRUCTIONS

1. Assemble each of the wooden sections of the frame according to the manufacturer's instructions. (Save the hinges and screws for later.) Sand any rough edges.

2. Cover your work surface with old newspapers. Use the medium-sized paintbrush to apply a coat of acrylic wood primer to both sides. Allow the primer to dry.

3. Paint the frame with one or two coats of the colored latex paint. Allow the paint to dry.

4. Apply a coat of protective wood sealer to the frame, and allow it to dry.

5. Hinge the screen (see pages 15 and 16 for instructions).

6. Spread the towel out on your work surface.

7. Measure the length between the dowel holes in the frame to determine the length of each panel. Cut three lengths of wax paper twice as long as this length plus 2 inches (5 cm). Mark off a 2-inch (5 cm) line on the end of each piece by creasing it and folding it back out. (This will serve as a tab for securing the bottom of each panel later on.) Fold the length of each paper in half (ending at the creased line) .

8. Open up one the papers, and position the half without the crease on top of the towel.

9. Cut out pieces of tissue paper and arrange them in a design of your choice on the wax paper, leaving a margin of at least 2 inches (5 cm) at both the bottom and the top of the paper. Fold the other half over the design. Align the edges, allowing the creased margin to extend beyond the folded paper.

10. Heat the iron to a medium setting. Place doubled newspaper on the wax paper, leaving a 2-inch-wide (5 cm) margin uncovered on each end (to use as a sleeve for each dowel). Slowly iron over the newspaper to fuse the papers together (avoiding the margins).

11. Lift the newspaper periodically to see if it's working. Don't leave the iron in one place too long. If wax stains appear on the newspaper, you've allowed the wax paper to get too hot.

12. Repeat steps 8 through 11 to create the remaining two paper panels.

1 3 . Slide a dowel through the closed sleeve on the top of each panel. Slide each dowel into the holes provided for it in the top of your frame.

1 4 . Insert the bottom dowels into the holes provided for them. Carefully pull the papers down to overlap the bottom dowels, pulling the creased tab to the back of the panel. Secure the tab with a line of hot glue.

Gallery

JULIE MORRINGELLO, *SCRITTURA SCREEN*. 2000.
60 x 40 x 12 IN. (150 x 100 x 30 CM). FRAME MADE OF WENGE CONTAIN-ING HAND-SCRIBED PLASTIC POLYETHYLENE COMPRESSED TO FORM A GENTLE CONVEX CURVE (ARTIST COLLABORATED WITH PAINTER EUGENE KOCH TO CREATE A TRANSPARENT SURFACE WHICH WAS SANDED AND "DRAWN" UPON); STAINLESS STEEL HARDWARE. PHOTO BY KEN WOISARD.

GIRL'S TREASURES SCREEN

THIS NONTRADITIONAL SCREEN IS MADE UP OF COMMON PLASTIC SLEEVES FILLED WITH THE SOME OF THE STUFF THAT GIRLS OFTEN LOVE TO SAVE SUCH AS TICKET STUBS, SUNGLASSES, GLITTER, NAILPOLISH, PHOTOS, AND SPECIAL NOTES. (WHETHER YOU'RE A GIRL OR NOT, YOU MAY FIND THIS IDEA IRRE-SISTIBLE!)

Materials & Tools

12 clear notebook-size, single-pocket plastic sleeves

13 clear notebook-size, four-pocket plastic sleeves (designed for holding film transparencies)

Scissors

Ruler

Fine-tip permanent marker

¼-inch (6 mm) hole punch

¼-inch (6 mm) two-part metal grommets, 100 count

Grommet setter with squeezable handles

Personal memorabilia such as photos, trinkets, ticket stubs, letters, small toys, etc.

50 1-inch-diameter (2.5 cm) metal binder rings (available at office supply stores)

Wire or curtain rod

Instructions

1. Use scissors to cut off the side tabs (made for holding them in a notebook) from each of the clear plastic sleeves.

2. Set aside two single-pocket sleeves and three four-pocket sleeves. On the remaining 20 sleeves, use the ruler and permanent marker to make marks 1½ inches (3.8 cm) in from each side and ½ inch (1.3 cm) from the top and bottom. On the five sleeves that you set aside, mark only the top of each, using the same measurements.

3. Use the hole punch to make holes through all of the marked points. Set the grommets into the bottom holes ONLY.

4. Place the five sleeves with no bottom marks in a horizontal row on the floor or a large work surface. Lay out the remaining sleeves above them to form vertical rows of five. Fill each of the pockets with personal items and memorabilia, keeping in mind the overall design of the screen as you arrange your items. Rearrange items as you wish.

5. Once you've filled all of the sleeves, attach the top grommets.

6. Use binder rings to connect each sleeve to the next so that you end up with five vertical columns. Suspend the sleeves next to one another with the top binder rings on your rod.

CRAIG VANDALL STEVENS, *SHOJI DOORS.* 2001. 80 x 72 IN. (200 x 180 CM). WHITE PINE SCREEN MADE WITH MORTISE-AND-TENON JOINERY; UNGLUED GRIDWORK HELD TOGETHER BY TIGHT-FITTING JOINERY; HAND-PLANED WOOD SURFACES; HAND-MADE PAPER APPLIED WITH GLUE MADE FROM WHITE RICE; SURFACE LEFT NATURAL. PHOTO BY STEPHEN WEBSTER.

NATURALLY INFLUENCED

Ever see a branch or twig that you just can't resist taking home? Or how about that brush pile in your backyard that looks so interesting that you can't bear to take it to the trash? This section shows you how to use some of those materials to make interesting screens. Or maybe you want to create the feeling of being outdoors by painting a screen with the image of a lush and embracing tree. Whatever your choices, nature is always the source of the most essential and significant expressions of beauty.

BAMBOO SCREEN WITH BRANCH POSTS

THE DESIGN OF THIS SCREEN INTE-GRATES KNOBBY, BRANCHED TREE LIMBS WITH THE STRAIGHT LINES OF TONKIN BAMBOO. FOR THE POSTS, THE ARTIST USED PEELED AND STAINED HEMLOCK LIMBS. CHOOSE STRAIGHT BRANCHES FOR THE HORIZONTAL PIECES OR STRINGERS—TWIST-ED ONES ARE MORE CHALLENGING!

Materials & Tools

Pruning saw

4 sturdy tree branches, each 64 inches (188 cm) long, 1½ inches (3.8 cm) in diameter, to serve as posts

Fine-toothed saw

Knife

Dark brown wood stain

Paintbrush

Polyurethane

Measuring tape

Fine-tip permanent marker

3 split lengths of bamboo, each 55 inches (139.7 cm) long, 2 inches (5.1 cm) in diameter, to serve as stringers

Quick-release clamps

Power drill and assorted drill bits

12 wood screws, each 2 inches (5.1 cm) long

Mason's cord

46 bamboo poles, each 43 inches (109.2 cm) long, 1 inch (2.5 cm) in diameter, to serve as verticals

138 wood screws, each 1¼ inches (3.2 cm) long

4 pieces of rebar, each 5 feet (1.5 m) long

Wire

Wire cutters

Black hemp twine (optional)

INSTRUCTIONS

1. Use the pruning saw to trim the tree branches. Use the fine-toothed saw to cut the tree branches and bamboo pieces to the lengths indicated.

2. Use the knife to peel the bark off the tree branches and scrape them to obtain a clean surface. Brush on several coats of the brown stain, let dry, then seal with the polyurethane.

3. Referring to figure 1 on page 139, mark the stringer placement on the posts. Measuring from the top of each post, make a mark at 14, 28, and 40 inches (35.6, 71.1, and 101.6 cm); the centers of the three stringers will cross the posts at these points. Make another mark at the bottom of each post, 44 inches (111.8 cm) from its top. This will help guide the position of the lowest end of the verticals. (There will be a 12-inch (30.5 cm) space between the verticals and the ground.)

4. On a flat surface, lay out the posts parallel to each other and 18 inches (45.7 cm) apart. Position the stringers across the posts at the marks you made, and clamp them in place. Use the power drill to make pilot holes, then drive in the 2-inch (5.1 cm) wood screws to secure the stringers to the posts. You've now formed the back of the fence framework.

5. Turn the fence framework over to the front side. Drive in 1¼ inch (3.2 cm) screws at the 44-inch (1 m) marks on the posts. Stretch lengths of mason's cord between the tops of the posts and the marks you made at the 44-inch (1 m) points on each post; the cord will serve as a guide to help you position the verticals straight across the stringers. Lay the verticals between the posts, and clamp them in place on the stringers. Use the drill to make pilot holes and to drive in the 1¼ inch (3.2 cm) screws, attaching the verticals to the stringers.

6. Place the split bamboo horizontals over the screw heads. If necessary, trim the ends to fit up against the end poles. At those points, drill pilot holes and use the 2½-inch (6.4 cm) screws to attach the horizontals to the verticals and stringers.

7. Now you'll install the screen fence. Mark the position of the posts at the intended site. Hammer the rebar twelve inches into the ground at these points, then posi-

tion the posts so they're snug
against the rebar. Use the wire or
string to tie the posts to the rebar
to stabilize the fence.

8 . If desired, use the black hemp
twine to make ornamental ties.

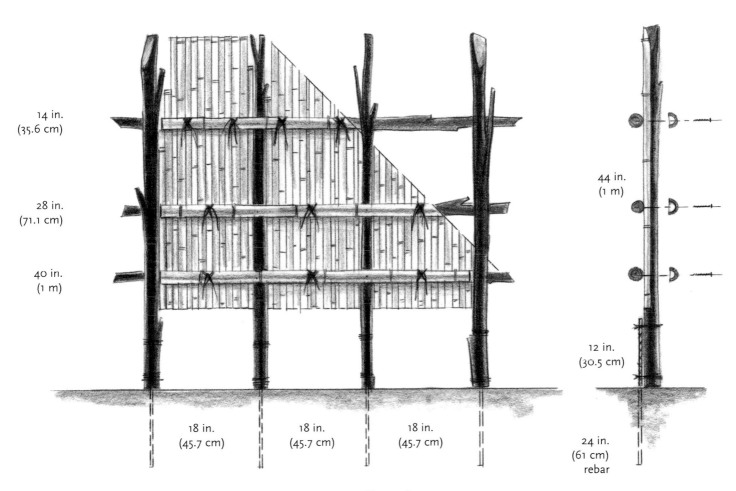

14 in.
(35.6 cm)

28 in.
(71.1 cm)

40 in.
(1 m)

18 in.
(45.7 cm)

18 in.
(45.7 cm)

18 in.
(45.7 cm)

44 in.
(1 m)

12 in.
(30.5 cm)

24 in.
(61 cm)
rebar

Figure 1

RUSTIC TWIG SCREEN

THIS SCREEN ALLOWS AIR AND LIGHT TO PASS THROUGH IT, WHILE DEFINING A SMALLER SPACE WITHIN A LARGE ONE. THE DESIGNER TRANSFORMED WOOD FROM BRUSH PILES AND YARD TRIMMINGS INTO A CONVERSATION PIECE.

INSTRUCTIONS

1 . Collect braches from brush piles and yard trimmings following the measurements given. Cut the branches to size with the pruning saw.

2 . Next you'll build the three sections of the screen, each composed of two uprights and four crosspieces. To assemble each section, lay the two uprights and the four crosspieces in position your workbench. Nail two crosspieces to the uprights, the first one 6 inches (15 cm) up from the bottom and the second one 6 inches (15 cm) down from the top. (Use the longest nails possible without the point emerging from the other side of the branch.)

3 . Turn the sections over.

4 . Arrange the four filler branches in each of the panels, and nail them into place. Nail the two remaining crosspieces to the uprights, sandwiching in the filler branches.

5 . Attach two leather hinges on either side of the middle screen, using two nails per hinge. The top and bottom hinges should be attached approximately 6 inches (15 cm) below the top and bottom crosspieces.

MATERIALS & TOOLS

6 branches, each measuring 6½ feet (1.9 m) long and approximately 2 inches (5 cm) in diameter, for the uprights

12 branches, each measuring 18 inches (45 cm), approximately 1 inch (2.5 cm) in diameter, for the crosspieces

12 lighter-weight branches, at least 6½ feet (1.9 m) long, for the panel fillers

Pruning saw

Large workbench (such as a piece of plywood on two sawhorses)

Assorted nails that range from 1½ to 3 inches (3.8 to 7.6 cm)

Hammer

Four leather pieces, cut to approximately 2 x 12 inches (5 x 30 cm), for hinging the panels

TWIG AND PAPER SCREEN

A DISCARDED TWIG SCREEN FOUND BY THIS DESIGNER WAS CONVERTED INTO AN OBJECT THAT PLAYFULLY CATCHES LIGHT ON BRIGHT PAPER WINDOWS.

INSTRUCTIONS

1. From the pieces of handmade paper, tear a selection of pieces that match the shape of the openings in the lattice on your screen panels, adding about a 1-inch (2.5 cm) margin to the edges of each piece. (Do not cut the pieces with scissors.)

2. Cover your work surface. Lay the screen flat on top of the covered surface.

3. In your container, mix 1 cup (.24 L) of PVA glue with an equal amount of water, or enough water to make a very thin, milk-like mixture.

4. Dip a piece of the paper into the diluted glue until it is saturated. Lay the paper on the matching opening on the screen, and press the edges around the twigs. Add as many pieces of paper as you like to make a design of your choice. Allow the paper to dry thoroughly.

5. If you want to further embellish the papers, tear smaller bits of paper and glue them on top of the affixed papers. Allow to dry.

MATERIALS & TOOLS

Small screen made of twigs with open latticework (available in craft and garden stores)

Heavy handmade papers with long natural fibers in colors of your choice

Old newspapers or drop cloth

Long flat food storage container, long casserole dish, or other container with room for dipping papers

PVA white archival glue made for paper

RUSTIC TWIG AND DOOR SCREEN

AN OLD WOODEN DOOR WITH LOTS OF HISTORY AND CHARACTER IS SOFT-ENED BY A SPLAY OF TWIGS ATTACHED TO THE SIDES.

Materials & Tools

Recycled/salvage wooden door

*Weathered wooden (salvage) board,
1 x 10 inches (2.5 x 25.4 cm) x
8 feet (2.4 m)*

*Weathered wooden (salvage) board,
1 x 6 inches (2.5 x 15.2 cm) x
8 feet (2.4 m)*

Bristle brush

Measuring tape

Circular saw

Protective gloves

Rag

*Wood stain (slightly lighter than the
wood you've chosen)*

Electric drill/screwdriver

Carpenter's square

*Drywall screws, #8 x 2½ inches
(6.4 cm)*

*4 to 6 tree limbs, each ¾ to 1¼
inches in diameter (1.9 x 3.2 cm)
x around 6 feet (1.8 m) long*

Handsaw or coping saw

24 six-penny (6d) finishing nails

Hammer

Instructions

1. Remove all the loose paint and dirt from the door and weathered wood boards with the bristle brush.

2. To create floor supports, use the circular saw to cut two 40-inch-long (1 m) pieces from the 1 x 10-inch (2.5 x 25.4 cm) x 8-foot (2.4 m) board. Across the cut end of each piece, measure in 1½ inches (3.8 cm) and make a mark. Then draw a 45° angle across the remaining width of the board. Use the saw to cut along these lines.

3. Put on protective gloves. Dip a rag in the wood stain, wring it out, and rub it on the freshly cut edges of each board to camouflage the cut edges.

4. Position your floor supports upright on a level surface as you want them to appear in the final piece, choosing which sides of the wood you'd like to face out and be seen. On the inside face of each support, draw a centerline across the WIDTH. Drill three pilot holes for your drywall screws that are evenly spaced along your line.

5. Position the door upright between the floor supports, and use the carpenter's square to make

sure that it is plumb (perfectly vertical). Through the pilot holes, drive screws through the supports and into the door.

6. Measure the distance between the two floor supports, and cut crosspieces from the 1 x 6-inch (2.5 x 15.2 cm) x 8-foot (2.4 m) board that match this length. Place the crosspieces flat between the supports on either side of the door, about 8 inches (20.3 cm) away from the door. From the face of the support, drill two horizontally aligned pilot holes that correspond with the butted end of each board. Attach the crosspieces with drywall screws.

7. Next, you'll attach branches. Start by holding the branches one-by-one against the sides of the door at an angle (see the finished photo of the project to see the effect that we created). Use your imagination! Your branches will lend their own special character to your piece.

8. Use a coping saw or handsaw to cut the branches so that they are a height that you like.

9. For each branch, position the butt end on the facing edging of the support (inside) along the top of the angled edge, extending the

branch across the narrow edge of the door behind it. From the face of the support, make a mark along the branch that follows the edge of the support. Use the coping saw or small handsaw to cut the branch along this line so that the butt end of the branch aligns with the angle of the support. Repeat this process to position, mark, and cut all the butt ends of the branches that you want to attach.

10. To attach the branches, drill a pilot hole for a finishing nail downward through each branch's butt end into the angled edge of the support. Drill another pilot hole from the side, through the branch where it crosses the door. Hammer a finishing nail through each pilot hole to attach each branch.

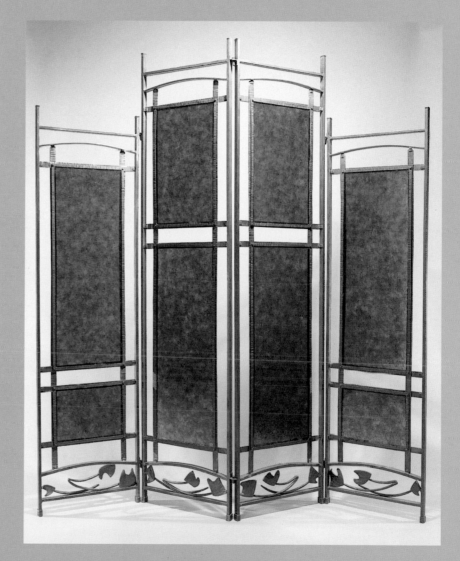

Susan Madacsi, *Peek-a-Boo Prairie Screen.* 2002. 7 x 6 ft. (2.1 x 1.8 m). Forged and fabricated steel frame with floral motif; mica panels. Photo by Joel Plesea.

LACED LEATHER SCREEN WITH STICK FRAME

This designer used sticks chewed by beavers to make the frame for this unusual piece. Hunt your own woods to find twigs or branches that draw your attention. construct a frame, Then fill it with stretched suede panels to make an eye-catching, suspended screen.

MATERIALS & TOOLS

4 sticks, as large or small as you want to create the frame for your screen

Medium-, fine-, and extra-fine sandpaper

Acrylic craft paint in brown and black

Medium-sized artist's paintbrush

Clean cotton cloth

Tung oil, clear polyurethane, or other wood sealer

Small C-clamps or large rubber bands (optional)

Electric drill with bit slightly smaller than diameter of screws

Screwdriver

4 sharp screws (such as drywall screws) long enough to fit about three-quarters of the way through each of the overlapping corners of your frame (You may need a couple of different lengths if your sticks are uneven.)

Four-ply waxed linen thread (available at craft or art stores that have bookbinding supplies)

Measuring tape

Piece(s) of suede in color(s) of your choice, large enough to fit singly or combined into your frame (available through leather suppliers, craft stores, and some fabric stores) *

Leather shears

Assorted rubber stamps

Acid-free, permanent ink pad

Awl and mallet or double-handled leather punch

Leather glue (for holding threads on back of suede)

Assorted beads and charms (optional)

*IF YOU'D LIKE TO SAVE TIME, CHOOSE ONE LARGE PIECE OF SUEDE TO FIT THE SIZE OF YOUR FRAME; OTHERWISE, BUY SMALLER PIECES OF SUEDE TO LACE TOGETHER INTO ONE PANEL (AS WAS DONE FOR THE SCREEN IN THIS PROJECT).

INSTRUCTIONS

1. If needed, cut or break your sticks or dowels so that they are of a size that can be overlapped to create the width and length of the frame you desire. (Keep in mind that the frame doesn't have to be a perfectly shaped one.)

2. Sand the sticks to remove the bark, working from the coarsest grade of sandpaper to the finest. After sanding, paint the sticks with brown and black acrylic paint, varying the color to create a natural look. Allow the paint to dry. (The sticks used for this project were sanded, painted black and brown, then lightly sanded again to highlight marks on the wood.)

3. Use the cotton cloth to rub a final coat of tung oil, clear polyurethane, or other wood sealer on the sticks. Allow it to dry.

4. On your work surface, position the sticks to form the frame for the screen, overlapping them to form corners. You may be able to use small C-clamps or large rubber bands to temporarily hold the sticks in place at the corners of the frame when you drill. (If your wooden pieces are too uneven for this, use a pencil to mark the points on each of the corners where the wooden pieces intersect. Mark the intersecting points on the front and on the corresponding piece of wood underneath. Then you can drill each stick independently.)

5. Use the electric drill fitted with the bit to drill a pilot hole through each of the corners through the top stick and through about half of the stick underneath. (Or, use your marks to do this if your sticks aren't clamped.)

6. From the front of the frame, use the screwdriver and screws to carefully screw the sticks together at each corner.

7. Cut off a long piece of waxed linen thread. Lash the corners of the frame where the sticks overlap by wrapping the cord several times on a diagonal between the sticks, leaving a piece of cord hanging on the back of the frame. Crisscross over to the other side of the "X" formed by the sticks, and wrap several times. Tie off the cord on the back.

8. Use a measuring tape to measure the width and length of the open space inside the frame (your frame will probably not be completely rectangular or square).

9. If you plan to use more than one panel, use the leather shears to cut pieces of suede that form one overall panel that fit together inside the frame, leaving a 1 to 1½-inch (2.5 to 3.8 cm) open space between the panel and the frame. If cutting one panel only, leave the same margin around the sides. (The suede will stretch slightly when you lace it to the frame.)

10. Spread out the suede panel or panel pieces on your work surface. Stamp an overall design on them with rubber stamps and permanent ink. (If the panel material you're using is thick enough, you may want to stamp the back of the panels as well.)

11. With the awl and mallet or a double-handled leather punch, pierce evenly spaced holes around the perimeter of each piece of suede, ¼ inch (6 mm) from each edge. To assemble more than one panel, cut off a long piece of waxed linen thread, and thread it by hand through the back of one of the holes along a butting edge, tying off the end on the back. (Use a bit of leather glue to hold the knot in place, if needed.) Lace the individual suede pieces together where they meet to form one

panel, continuing to tie the threads off on the back as needed.

12. Place the frame on your work surface, and position the panel inside it. Cut off a long piece of waxed linen, and loosely tie one end of it to the frame with a square knot. Loosely lace the panel to the frame along ONE SIDE ONLY, leaving a space slightly narrower than what you allowed when you cut the suede. When you reach the end of the first side, tie it off with a knot.

13. Lace the opposite side of the frame, pulling the suede gently so that it floats in the frame, but without damaging the holes. Repeat this process to lace the remaining two sides, so that the suede is stretched lightly in the frame. If you need to untie a knot and make the lace tighter, do so and gently pull the linen threads along the length of the side to take up any slack.

14. When you are satisfied with the lacing, tie all the knots firmly with square knots, and trim any loose ends.

15. As an optional step, tie extra lengths of waxed linen from the top of the frame, and slide beads or charms onto the strings,

tying them off at different lengths.

16. To hang your screen, make loops as long as you need from the waxed linen for the top corners of the frame. For each loop, cut a length of waxed linen, double it over, and make a knot in each of the ends. Use a weaver's knot to attach each hang loop to a corner of the frame.

DESIGNER: SUSAN MCBRIDE

TREE OF LIFE SCREEN

INSPIRED BY A TREE OF LIFE THEME AND FOLK ART, THIS ARTIST USED A WIDE, CURVED SCREEN TO PROJECT THE LIMBS OF AN EMBRACING TREE. SHE CARVED HER OWN STAMPS TO PRINT THE BIRDS AND LEAVES BEFORE DEFINING THEM FURTHER WITH DELICATE, PAINTED BRUSHSTROKES.

Materials & Tools

3 sheets of ¾-inch (1.9 cm) x 4 x 8-foot (1.2 x 2.4 m) smooth plywood (you'll cut the central panel from one sheet and the two side panels from the other sheet)

Sawhorses and large sheet of plywood or other large work surface

Pencil

Long piece of string

Jigsaw

C-clamps

Fine- and medium-grit sandpaper

Small handheld sander (optional)

Tack cloth

Drop cloth

3 paint rollers

Paint tray with disposable liners

Latex primer

Flat interior latex paint in light blue

Flat interior latex paint in dark brown

1-inch-wide (2.5 cm) flat paint-brush

Small paint roller or sponge

Artists' acrylic paints in a range of colors (white, light blue, light yellow, light green, dark green, several shades of blue, burnt sienna, vermillion, and yellow ochre)

Artist's palette or large sheet of glass for mixing paints

Piece of chalk or soft pencil

CONTINUED ON NEXT PAGE

Instructions

1. Cut one of the sheets of plywood in half lengthwise. On the floor or your work surface, flank the remaining sheet of plywood with the two pieces, lining them up lengthwise. Use a pencil attached at the tip to a length of string as a large compass for drawing the top of the panels, attaching the end of the string with a pushpin or nail at the point shown in figure 1 below. Draw an arc across the top of the panels. On your work surface, use the jigsaw to cut out the wood panels following the curved lines.

2. Lightly sand the edges, fronts, and backs of each panel, and wipe them down with the tack cloth to remove the dust.

3. Cover the floor of your work space with the drop cloth, and lay out the panels. Use one of the paint rollers to cover them with a coat of primer. Allow each side to dry thoroughly.

4. Use the second roller to apply two coats of the light blue latex paint to one side of the screen. Allow the paint to dry. Flip the panels over.

5. Roll the other side of the screen with two coats of dark brown latex paint, and allow it to dry. Use the 1-inch (2.5 cm) paintbrush to paint the sides of the panels dark brown. Allow the paint to dry, and flip the panels back over, lining them up so that the straight edges are butted together.

6. Squeeze some white paint onto your palette. Use the small roller or sponge to paint large, soft clouds on the blue background. Allow the paint to dry.

7. Use chalk or a pencil to sketch the tree design (see figure 2 on

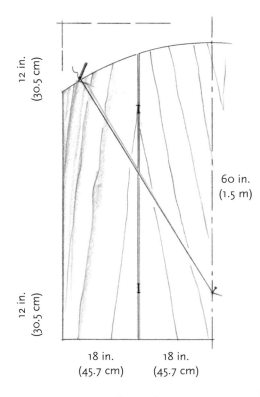

Centerline

12 in.
(30.5 cm)

60 in.
(1.5 m)

12 in.
(30.5 cm)

18 in.
(45.7 cm)

18 in.
(45.7 cm)

Figure 1

page 156) onto the three panels, extending the limbs out onto the side panels.

8. Squeeze out paints onto your palette. Add a bit of matt medium to the paint as you work to keep it fresh. Paint the trunk and branches of the tree with layers of acrylic paint in a variety of colors. Highlight the branches and trunk with brighter shades of paint. (Don't overdo the addition of white to your paints, it will dull them.) Allow the paint to dry completely.

9. You have several options for painting the birds and leaves. We choose to carve our own rubber stamps so that the images could be reused and repeated on the panels (see steps 10 through 13 if you want to do this). You can also use purchased rubber stamps of birds and leaves.

10. To carve your own stamps, begin by looking at the designs in figure 3 on page 156, or make sketches of your own in pencil. Keep in mind that each image you use will be reversed when it is printed.

11. Transfer each of the images you plan to use onto the rubber carving blocks using one of two methods: Use the soft graphite pencil to rub back and forth across the back of each piece of paper containing an image before taping it to a rubber block, or place graphite paper facedown on the rubber block followed by the image. With gentle, steady pressure, trace each image with a ball-point pen onto each block.

12. Use the black marker to outline the image after you've traced it, making it easier to see as you carve it.

13. Carve each bird or leaf design into the rubber carving block using the large blades to clear out open spaces and the small blades for detailed work. (Keep in mind that the carved-out portions of the block will not be printed and the areas left standing will print the image.) Carve off the edges of the block with the craft knife so that they won't print on the design.

14. Before stamping or painting the birds, use a sea sponge to apply a lighter blue to the background where you plan to print each bird. This will create a soft background for the image.

15. If you're stamping instead

Materials & Tools

Paintbrushes in a variety of sizes

Jar of acrylic matte medium

Bird and leaf designs, if carving stamps (see fig. 3, page 156 for examples)

Bird and leaf rubber stamps (optional)

Soft graphite pencil or graphite paper (optional)

Masking tape (optional)

Rubber carving blocks in a variety of sizes (optional)

Ballpoint pen (optional)

Black fine-tipped marker (optional)

Set of linoleum cutting tools for carving blocks (optional)

Craft knife (optional)

Sea sponge

Foam brayer

Colored pencils (optional)

4-inch-wide (10.2 cm) flat paint-brush

6 double-acting/butterfly hinges with screws, each hinge measuring ¾ x 1¾ inches (1.9 x 4.4 cm)

Electric drill/screwdriver

15. If you're stamping instead of painting, use a foam brayer to roll dark shades of acrylic paint onto the bird stamps, and press the stamps onto the screen where you wish them to appear. (Because acrylic paints dry quickly, rinse each stamp with warm water to remove the paint between printings.) Alternate light and dark greens for printing the surrounding leaves.

16. After stamping, you can add more painted details to each image with acrylic paints and colored pencils, using the stamped image as guide. Or, if you prefer the rough look of the stamped image, there's no need to add much more detail.

17. After the paint has dried, use the large paintbrush to apply a coat of the acrylic matte medium to the entire screen.

18. Hinge the screen (see pages 15 and 16 for instructions).

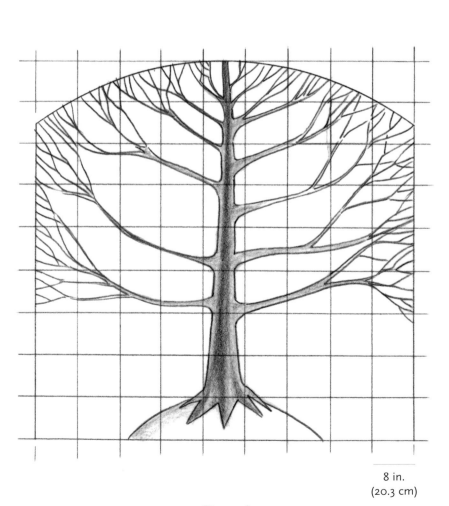

8 in.
(20.3 cm)

Figure 2

Figure 3

DESIGNER: KATHERINE AIMONE;
PAINTINGS BY STEVE AIMONE

MOVEABLE GALLERY SCREEN

H INGE TOGETHER HOLLOW-CORE DOORS THAT YOU'VE PAINTED TO CREATE A FREESTAND-ING SCREEN TO HOLD YOUR FAVORITE ARTWORK. THIS ARTIST WAS INSPIRED TO PAINT A SERIES OF SKY PAINTINGS FOR THIS SCREEN.

INSTRUCTIONS

1. Place the drop cloth on the floor or your work surface. Use the paint roller and paintbrush to prime the fronts and the sides of the doors with a coat of latex primer. Allow the primer to dry before priming the other sides of the doors.

2. Use a clean roller to apply the off white paint to all surfaces of the doors. Allow the paint to dry thoroughly.

3. Hinge the screen (see pages 15 and 16 for instructions).

4. Stand the doors up. Tilt the panels against a wall with the screen open so that you can hang the artwork.

5. Decide on an arrangement of artwork that works on the four panels. Think of the panels as one piece, and be sensitive to the relationship between the pieces that you plan to hang. (You can stack several pieces on each panel if you wish.)

6. Hang the pieces with hangers or nails. (You can also hang another "gallery" on the reverse side if you want.)

MATERIALS & TOOLS

4 hollow-core doors, each 18 inches (45.7 cm) wide

Drop cloth

2 paint rollers

Paint tray

1-inch-wide (2.5 cm) paintbrush

Latex primer

Off-white semigloss interior latex paint

6 double-acting, butterfly screws, each hinge measuring ¾ x 1¾ inches (1.9 x 4.4 cm)

Electric drill/screwdriver

Selected pieces of artwork (paintings, prints, photographs, drawings, or other two-dimensional art) that fit the width of the panels

Picture hangers or nails

Hammer

Designers

REBECCA S. ARMSTRONG (Asheville, NC) is a sculptor, weaver, knitter, and bookbinder who graduated from Yale University with a degree in sculpture. **LYNA FARKAS** (Asheville, NC) is a teacher, consultant, and artisan in the field of decorative painting and restoration. She is a graduate of the City and Guilds of London and owns a business called *In the Spirit of Decorum*. **DANA IRWIN** (Asheville, NC) is an fine artist, illustrator, and designer. She has worked as an art director for Lark Books for 15 years and is coauthor of Lark's *Salvage Style for the Garden*. **LOREN KNOUSE** (Asheville, NC) is a furniture designer and maker whose emphasis is on using architectural salvage materials. His work is sold nationally. **KIM HODGES** (Asheville, NC) has worked as a professional artist for more than eight years. Her paintings and home accents produced by her company called Queen's Crescent can be found in hundreds of stores and galleries. **DIANA LIGHT** (Weaverville, NC) is a general designer who has created projects for many Lark

books. She is the coauthor of Lark's *The Weekend Crafter: Etching Glass*. **DOUGLAS MADARAS** (Asheville, NC) designs commercial interiors for restaurants and other spaces, emphasizing the use of salvaged items. His work is on the Web at madarasdesigns.com. **SUSAN MCBRIDE** (Asheville, North Carolina) is a graphic artist who designs books, logos, and brochures. In her spare time, she loves to paint, carve rubber stamps, and garden. **MICHAEL MOONEY** (Asheville, NC) is a custom home builder who specializes in green building techniques. His work can be found at Sky People Gallery and Design Studio in Asheville. **MICHELLE NEWMAN** (San Antonio, TX and South Beach, FL) is a multi-media designer whose emphasis in on clothing and fiber. Her work has been published in numerous magazines and shown on television, including the *Discovery Channel*. **CORI SARACENI** (Barnardsville, NC) is a fiber artist who creates woven metal sculptures. Her work is in the collections of corporations and museums. **NEIL SPENCER** (Weaverville, NC) is the Director of Interactive Sales for an Asheville-based healthcare marketing company. His lives with his fiancé, Reagan, who is an artist. **TERRY TAYLOR** (Asheville, NC) is a multi-media artist who works as an editor and project designer for Lark Books. **CHARLENE THOMAS** (Tavares, FL) paints abstract compositions inspired by poetry, life experiences, dreams, and daily observations. She also writes haiku poetry and has published a book of her writing called *The Spiral Arranger* (1995). **LUANNE UDELL** (Keene, NH) is a nationally-exhibited mixed media artist. She recently published Lark's *The Weekend Crafter: Rubber Stamp Carving*. **RICKIE WESBROOKS** (Asheville, NC) is an active fiber artist who is currently designing woven fabrics for the textile industry. He also does textile conservation and restoration. His small-format tapestries are exhibited nationally.